Facing Financial Exigency

Facing Financial Exigency

Strategies for Educational Administrators

Frank R. Kemerer
Ronald P. Satryb

State University of New York

Lexington Books
D.C. Heath and Company
Lexington, Massachusetts
Toronto

Library of Congress Cataloging in Publication Data

Main entry under title:

Facing financial exigency.

Includes index.
1. Education—New York (State)—Finance. 2. Collective bargaining—Teachers—New York (State). I. Kemerer, Frank R. II. Satryb, Ronald P.
LB2826.N7F32   379'152'09747   76-45606
ISBN 0-669-01114-2

Published simultaneously in Canada.

Printed in the United States of America.

International Standard Book Number: 0-669-01114-2

Library of Congress Catalog Card Number: 76-45606

To those present and future administrators who struggle to keep their institutions fiscally sound and educationally viable in hard times.

Contents

List of Figures and Tables

Preface

Financial exigency appears certain to spread across the educational landscape and to require the attention of administrators for some time to come. It is just as certain that prepared administrators will be able to maximize the opportunities financial exigency offers for a rebirth of institutional purpose and in the process minimize the trauma of adjusting institutions to the realities of the 1980s and 1990s. What is called for are rational, constructive, and humanistic management strategies in the face of extreme and conflicting pressures.

This book is designed to help those responsible for the effective and efficient use of personnel, plant, and equipment to adapt their institutions to times of fiscal stringency. It is meant for educational administrators at all levels of education, particularly those in postsecondary education. It is also meant for those who teach and research educational administration and for their students. As administrators in the troubled state of New York in the mid 1970s, we feel in a unique position to identify critical components of financial exigency and to call upon acknowledged experts to provide insights and strategies for coping with them.

This book differs from others directed to educational administrators in two important respects. It has an overarching theme of financial exigency that runs through all the chapters. And it is designed to be pragmatic and experiential. We asked our contributors to write what they think administrators must know about their subject as it relates to financial exigency. We have purposely avoided including topics that already command substantial attention in the literature. Thus, for example, fund-raising procedures and budgetary processes are not included except in a tangential manner. For topics that are included, we asked that maximum emphasis be placed on lessons of experience.

Our contributors are to be congratulated for their complete cooperation in writing these chapters to our specifications and meeting the deadlines we set. Thanks must also go to our colleagues who served as readers for this project: Robert W. MacVittie, Hugh Hammett, Bruce Ristow, and James Young. Finally, we owe a special debt of gratitude to our typist, Luella Schumaker, and our hard-working secretaries, Susan Urbanczyk and Lenora McMaster.

Frank R. Kemerer
Ronald P. Satryb

Geneseo, New York

Introduction: Challenges and Opportunities

We know from experience that the crisis in education called "financial exigency" can have drastic consequences for people as well as for institutions. Students find courses, programs, and services cancelled. Faculty members find themselves in the clutches of retrenchment with little hope of establishing a new career. Institutions may even be faced with extinction. At the City University of New York, for example, 1975-76 brought plans for restructuring the entire CUNY system into a fewer number of institutions with fewer faculty and staff members. More faculty members were laid off at CUNY that year than at any other institution in the history of higher education. It is not easy to retrench over 1100 faculty members outright and not feel the brutal, almost inhuman nature of the task.

At the same time, financial exigency presents a unique opportunity. Some have maintained that the proliferation of institutions and duplication of programs in the 1950s and 1960s left much of the educational establishment overbuilt and inefficient. Nothing forces change as quickly as hard times. Many institutions are left with little choice but to cut expenses, search for new markets and missions, and hope to outdo the competition. Financial exigency may thus be a catalyst for institutional adjustment to the realities of our times. As such, it could represent a positive force.

It is impossible, of course, to talk meaningfully about financial exigency without defining the term. We called upon an expert to provide us with an economic and legal framework for understanding what financial exigency is all about. In Chapter 1, David Leslie undertakes this task. Having a better grasp of the subtleties of financial exigency, the reader will find the second chapter by Stephen Finn and William Proctor of value in providing insight about the kind of management structure and practices necessary to cope successfully with financial exigency. We realize too infrequently how haphazardly the administrative constituency has been constructed and operated in almost all levels and types of educational institutions.

We asked William Collard, James Farmer, and John Harrison in Chapter 3 to candidly assess the value and importance of management and planning systems to educational institutions in general. Do the systems provide sufficient benefit to be worth the cost, and, if so, what types of systems are available? In Chapter 4, Frank R. Kemerer investigates a problem of growing concern to administrators, particularly in postsecondary education, struggling with academic collective bargaining: How does one cope with union demands for power to influence personnel and programmatic decisions, largely brought about by financial exigency? In the next chapter, Ronald P. Satryb provides a strategy for actually excising personnel and programs. Retrenchment presents the greatest challenge to campus administrators. If handled badly, retrenchment will produce waves of conflict in the form of votes of no-confidence, grievances, court actions, and never-ending recriminations. Even if handled as rationally and humanistically as possible, retrenchment will never be easy to carry out. But as Satryb suggests, a well-developed strategy can go a long way toward keeping conflict manageable and yet protect the integrity of the institution.

J. Victor Baldridge provides valuable insight into change processes in Chapter 6, noting that innovation is seriously threatened by financial exigency in a number of ways. Baldridge's chapter provides the strategies essential for administrators to respond fully to financial exigency by seizing the opportunity it presents to encourage beneficial reform.

With Chapter 7, the focus of the book shifts off campus in progressively wider circles. In Chapter 7, George W. Angell criticizes higher educational administrators for their timidity in entering the legislative arena, the place where the battles over financial exigency are initially fought. He describes in detail the kind of positive action administrators should take to provide their institutions with security from negative legislative and public action. Chapter 8 is written by two masters of the regional consortia movement, Fritz H. Grupe and Alexander Cameron, themselves directors of consortia of postsecondary institutions. They suggest that voluntary regional consortia offer the best avenue for interinstitutional cooperation and coordination beneficial both to institutions experiencing financial exigency and to the needs of the communities institutions serve. But for consortia to provide benefits that outweigh costs, administrators must be willing to surrender a measure of institutional autonomy. Without such a commitment, regionalism may prove unworkable in times of financial exigency.

In the final chapter, Patrick Callan and Richard Jonsen present the case for statewide coordination. They note that it is essential for state legislatures to develop a constructive policy for dealing with the needs of the private sector as well as with the public. They describe the tasks statewide coordinating boards will have to perform in the future and point out the challenges these agencies must master if they are to function in the best interests of all of postsecondary education and of the general public.

Public and private elementary and secondary school administrators will find many of these chapters speaking directly to their needs, as well as to those of their postsecondary colleagues. The first six chapters are particularly effective in addressing the concerns of all educational administrators, regardless of the type of institution they manage.

We are confident that this is one book administrators will wish to keep within ready reach as they struggle with the problems of an uncertain future. It is to them that this book is dedicated.

Facing Financial Exigency

Introduction to Chapter 1

What is financial exigency? Most educators have trouble pronouncing it, to say nothing about understanding its meaning and implications for education. We asked David Leslie, a frequent commentator on topics of critical concern to administrators, to draw upon his research at the University of Virginia to provide us with a comprehensive examination of financial exigency. His introductory chapter is thus particularly relevant to all that follows, since the exact meaning of financial exigency is currently a topic of heated debate among administrators, professional organizations, faculty unions, and courts.

In Chapter 1, Leslie explores the nature of financial exigency, as well as the conditions under which it is said to exist. He provides models for identifying institutional stress that lead to fiscal crisis and looks at the impact of financial exigency on institutional mission and goals, academic values, structural change, the political climate for education, and innovation and change. This chapter is thus a fitting introduction to the remaining eight chapters, which examine many of these concerns in depth and provide strategies for coping with them.

1

Financial Exigency and the Future of the Academy

David W. Leslie

Financial exigency is a complicated and immediate threat to a substantial number of colleges and universities in the United States. In raw terms, it is a money crisis. But it is more. A financial exigency is a crisis of purpose, a crisis of authority, a crisis of finance, a crisis of management, and a crisis of spirit. Resolution of exigency can only occur when this complex set of factors is addressed directly and simultaneously. This chapter will describe the roots of straitened financial position, the possible impacts on the character of higher education, and options for the future.

Defining Exigency

An "exigency" is a set of conditions that steal quietly into the structure and fabric of institutional life, making themselves felt in increasingly painful fashion until important constituents finally admit the need for change. The important criterion in reaching a practical definition of exigency is to locate the threshhold of stress beyond which the need for change is clear. This is an educational, political, and legal question as much as an economic one. There is seldom an a priori consensus about where this threshhold lies, and the experience of each institution is the standard against which any definition must be judged.

Measuring Financial Health

To date, no real consensus exists on a set of standardized measures of financial health. Accounting procedures differ from one institution to the next, meaning that reliably defined measures are unavailable. One cannot be confident about cross-institutional comparisons, nor can one assume that data on a particular institution are consistent over time. Even if one had reliable data, there remains a significant question over where to find a meaningful bottom line that will serve as an index. The pressing issue over measurement means that for the present there is only limited capacity to project future states. Consequently, there is no firm consensus about whether higher education is heading for a new boom, a steady state, or a long-term retrenchment.

The common indices are, naturally, income and its real growth, expenditures and their real growth, enrollment (demand) patterns, and ratios of selected components of each. In the end, only a longitudinal, multivariate study such as the New Jersey Commission on Financing Postsecondary Education has undertaken will provide the essential experience with and refinement of measures required to make useful diagnoses of current conditions and projections of future trends.[1]

For any local situation, though, the weighting of components before assessing ratios in the income-expenditure matrix is essential to diagnosis. Grossly measured trends probably yield dangerously uninformative and simplistic analyses. Using enrollment patterns as an example, one may find a relatively "healthy" situation in steadily increasing numbers. But body counts may fail to detect increasing numbers of part-time students and the implications for tuition receipts. Softness in specific program areas may remain hidden also. Applications-to-enrollments may be a declining ratio for some programs, while (real) cost per credit hour may be an increasing ratio for the same programs. In other words, one program may be lagging behind institutional productivity indexes and suffering from declining demand even though actual body count enrollment holds constant or increases. The "health" of any given program or institution is patently *not* measurable by a single index. And no quantitative measures *alone* will detect subtle qualitative shifts that are made as colleges compromise to stay afloat.

Contemporary Studies

Existent studies of institutional financial condition provide either *relative* definitions of stress (some institutions are worse off than others), *subjective* definitions (the feeling of exigency is real), or *circular* definitions (cuts have been made, so exigency exists). The recently published study by the New Jersey commission employed an essentially relative definition; a panel of experts ranked the overall financial condition of a sample of institutions on a five-point scale. The condition of any institution can now be compared statistically to the condition of this sample and labelled with a position on the scale. Cheit's analysis of financial circumstances at forty-one colleges used a combination of self-report (the subjective definition) and indicators of actual program cuts to identify institutions headed for or actually experiencing financial difficulty.[2] More often, analyses have been macroeconomic in scope, arriving at sweeping generalizations about the plight of one sector or another—or of higher education as a whole—without clearly providing measurable and meaningful threshholds of exigency against which one might assess the condition of a particular institution.

At present, then, the science of measuring institutional financial health is primitive. There is disagreement over how to measure financial condition, and longitudinal data do not yet exist in a form that will permit reliable trend analyses. It is not even certain that projection from past experience is possible;

fundamental dislocations in purpose, governance, and financing may have changed the very quality of the enterprise.

Given, then, that no quantitative definition of exigency is available, one turns to usage of the term to see what it means. Once again, however, it will be apparent that a standardized definition does not emerge.

The State of the Law

One line can be drawn with some confidence; an institution might demonstrate sufficient distress to qualify for bankruptcy proceedings. Liquidation of assets, corporate reorganization in receivership, or, in extremis, corporate death can result. The financial stresses normally encountered are seldom so reflective of imprudence in the management of income and assets.

Legally, the issue of when and how an institution can or must take action to cut losses is essentially a matter of local policy and of interpretation of its various contractual obligations. The most important contractual relationships affecting retrenchment plans are those with the faculty (individually or collectively). While litigation of faculty employment rights has not been especially helpful in constructing a definition of exigency, some guidelines can be drawn.

The most important case bearing on a definition of the line a college must cross before "stress" can justify action against faculty with property rights to their positions is *AAUP, Bloomfield College Chapter* v. *Bloomfield College*. A New Jersey appellate court, sustaining the trial court's holding against the college, ruled on the standards that should be employed in testing the facts. In general, the result makes these points clear:

1. The college must make a showing of stress defined as "a state of urgency." A lack of liquidity or insufficient cash flow is an acceptable standard.
2. The court may not substitute its judgment for a good faith determination on the question by the trustees of the institution as to sufficient liquidity. (One presumes that any evidence will have to meet criteria of responsible accounting procedures, though.)
3. The college's burden is to show both a bona fide state of urgency and to show by a preponderance of the evidence that the specific dismissals undertaken were a direct result of the college's financial condition.[3]

Where tenured faculty are involved, the college's burden does not stop with the demonstration of stress. It must present a convincing (although not airtight) case explaining and justifying the reasons for each dismissal. (Bloomfield College, the court held, had failed to meet this latter burden.) In other words, it may be easier for the college to *assert* exigency than to *correct it* by abrogating contracts. For example, a Nebraska state college board budget recently authorized eighty positions at an institution with ninety-nine faculty. A tenured professor at this institution who had been dismissed won an award of back pay because the college had erred procedurally when acting against him.[4]

But for all the litigation generated in recent years over retrenchment, the critical threshhold of stress has not been defined exactly. Typically, the existence of stress has been stipulated by the parties to the suit and litigation has focused on procedure or substantive contractual rights as protection against admittedly legitimate cuts. As a result, it is difficult to establish a clear and widely applicable line over which "trouble" lurks. Certainly, an operating surplus in one year does not mean security, nor does a deficit mean chaos. In short, "exigency" is a term of art or one that takes on meaning as the evolution of circumstances give it shape and content.

It is clear that the AAUP does not accept an operating deficit *by itself* as indicative of an exigency severe enough to justify personnel retrenchment. The AAUP *amicus* brief in *Lumpert* v. *University of Dubuque* argued that the phrase "bona fide" in its regulations was specifically intended to protect tenured faculty against retrenchment moves taken by deficit-ridden colleges in the depression era. Instead of relying on an operating deficit, the AAUP urges an assessment of "the entire financial picture" of the college and a direct effort to relate that picture to its educational mission: "The real touchstone for analysis is the institution's ability to perform its educational mission without serious diminution of quality."[5]

The question in this view is how the nature of the exigency relates to specific sectors of the budget and what actions can be taken directly to relieve the stress. Stress that stems from a budget ceiling imposed by a legislature is different from stress caused by declining enrollment. Solutions to either condition require markedly different assumptions; economic conditions may make the state budget problem a short-lived one, but more permanent change of a cultural sort may underlie shifting enrollment patterns.

The AAUP guidelines require consensual definition of exigency rather than detection of any absolute syndrome. The whole process of declaring and adapting to exigency is to be a collaborative one with faculty and administrators asserting prime influence in their respective areas of competence and responsibility. The *Lumpert* brief expands on the rationale for this aspect of the regulations:

[Judicial review] is facilitated to the extent the agency can show that its expertise was really brought to bear, i.e., that it weighed all the relevant factors and indicators in a responsible fashion. The greater an institutional consensus on the dimensions of an exigency and the need to terminate particular appointments in response thereto, the greater also is the likelihood of bona fides; thus, the greater the consensus the less likely that the decision is arbitrary or that the administration is using the financial condition as a subterfuge and the less the court is required to assess the decision itself.[6]

Although there may be no legal basis for faculty participation in retrenchment decisions, there are important reasons to encourage it. Petersen points out the failure of the Bloomfield College administration to demonstrate "good faith" in diagnosing and treating its financial woes. He goes on to suggest that faculty participation should serve as an important judicial index to good faith.[7] A meaningful faculty role would, in this theory of good faith, go a long way toward persuading judges that retrenchment decisions had been made in a nonarbitrary, noncapricious, nonvindictive way.

In any case, standard practice appears to leave the definition of exigency to a situational decision process: Exigency will be defined by the facts as they appear. The responsible and affected parties will collectively agree on the degree of urgency that exists and collaboratively define the need for and form of correction action. This general approach appears to be the most common one, as indicated by searches of collective bargaining agreements and institutional policy statements. For the most part, existing policy statements spell out the procedures for reaching a mutually satisfactory conclusion that an exigency exists, but they stop short of stating precisely what conditions define an exigent state.

Given that assessment strategies need considerable development, Cheit discussed evaluation of financial health in decidedly philosophical terms. He suggests that the dependent variable in studies of financial health should be the institution's ability to carry out its mission. Indeed, that is exactly the standard he employed in his well-known study; whenever quality standards were reduced or programs cut, he inferred financial difficulty was present.

There are no narrow statistical or legal standards to use in deciding issues of program quality or importance. These are professional and institutional standards, and they may dictate sacrificing a great deal for the sake of particular purposes. In raw terms, the threshhold of exigency may be much higher where the purposes and value of particular activities are clear; a college does not give up things it knows to be at the very core of its existence just because it is financially difficult to proceed. Highly purposeful, valuable, and effective colleges have persisted for decades under straitened conditions that would elsewhere have long since prompted "retrenchment." The great strength of many financially weak colleges lies in the commitment of their trustees, faculty, students, alumni, and friends to the idea of the college rather than to its balance sheet. Quiet sacrifices, long commitments, and close involvements have gone further to sustain the church-related colleges, the black colleges, and the special-purpose colleges than has any real degree of financial security. The preservation of traditions, cultures, and revered modes of educational experience simply outweighs money in importance on some scales of value. So the roots of exigency may lie as much in the commitment of people as in the flow of dollars.

Roots of Financial Exigency

One resists enumerating the "causes" of a state of affairs so imprecisely defined as exigency. Hence, this section will focus on *hypothesized* conditions leading to financial trouble. One major premise is that financial trouble is essentially a symptom of accumulated problems and results from their interaction or compounding over time. An allied premise is that the roots of financial trouble differ from one institution to the next—or surely from one type of institution to another.

Externally: An End to Growth

Overlaying these unique institutional conditions, certain broad national patterns pushing many colleges to or over the brink of financial trouble in the 1970s seem a matter of consensus. Expanding ambitions and commitments long fueled by a commensurate rise in proportion of the gross national product devoted to higher education have evidently hit a ceiling. The momentum of expansion has simply outlasted the elastic capacity of the national economy to absorb and pay for it. In simpler terms, scarce resources were needed elsewhere for evidently more pressing things. Families hard hit by inflation redirected cash and borrowing power to consumption, higher interest rates, and investments that began to appear relatively sounder than a devalued college degree. State and local governments became simultaneously pressed by rapid inflation, increased unemployment, and inelasticity in their (sometimes shrinking) tax bases. Federal outlays for various higher education programs withered under pressure from the political interests of Congress and the executive. Endowment funds were crippled by an inopportune choice of more liberal investment strategies at a time of reversals in precisely the markets the new approaches were designed to tap.

As these serious weaknesses all developed together in the bases for support of higher education, costs were escalating. Operating expenses were boosted quickly by high annual inflation rates, making budgets and plans look grossly unrealistic in short periods of time. Administrative costs were escalated by increasingly stringent and elaborate accountability mechanisms that emerged from state-level coordinating bodies and federal concerns for individual rights. Capital spending projects suffered from overruns. The cost of security for plant and personnel in the various forms of insurance surged under pressure of student unrest, plant deterioration, changes in the legal parameters of liability for public agencies and charitable corporations, increasing costs of settlement, skyrocketing costs of medical care, and crises in unemployment funds. Low faculty turnover resulted in ever higher proportions of tenured appointments, meaning higher levels of long-term financial commitments. Caught between weakening support and escalating costs, colleges found their markets turning softer. Tuitions were discounted indirectly via various financial aid plans and enrollment figures turned fickle, if not actually sour.

Thus, the national economic dislocations of the 1970s brought acute crises—financial exigencies—to significant numbers of American colleges. Commitments could not be met and cuts had to be made. This view backward is merely simplistic hindsight, however. It is clear that individual institutions were brought to their fiscal knees by widely varying conditions. For some institutions, the recent past is prologue to chronic ill health and grim prospects for the future.

Internally: Models of Stress

Before the nature and extent of fiscal crisis in a given college can be dealt with, its specific roots have to be identified. Balderston has outlined five predictable "models of financial stress," allowing that "any one institution may have some combination of these stresses accumulating at the same time."[8] He labels the models "expanded aspiration, time passing, stabilization after growth, conscientious overcommitment, and income tapering."

The first model of stress ("expanded aspiration") has its roots, Balderston suggests, in the level of investment committed to new and higher level programs. The New Jersey commission report suggests that this form of stress afflicts private institutions that have sought to expand clienteles by adding graduate programs. Evidently, the potential market for these degrees has suffered due to competition in price from the expanding public sector and competition in quality from established universities.

The second model of stress ("time passing") is based on the ordinary rise in "fixed commitment." Balderston uses faculty salaries, maintenance, and overhead as examples of inevitably rising costs. While all institutions will suffer from some degree of this stress, the smaller, more stable colleges are perhaps most vulnerable. Obsolescing plant, aging faculty, and the inability to benefit from economies of scale lock institutional fortunes into rigid cost spirals that will outstrip "industry-wide" standards. Tuition is raised in response, and markets shrink from noncompetitive programs and prices.

"Stabilization after growth" produces a period of static real income that must be spread to cover hidden long-term costs associated with expansion. Probably most afflicted with this syndrome are the public institutions, particularly ambitious universities, which suddenly must face legislated or administratively ordered enrollment ceilings. Investments in facilities and faculty to generate further growth now turn into liabilities because that growth cannot occur.

"Conscientious overcommitment" as a source of stress develops, Balderston suggests, out of commitments to poor students, students who need remedial attention, and extensive service to communities. While arising from moral and educational convictions, these commitments have inflated student aid budgets, decreased efficiency, and generally extended the available resources of many institutions. One suspects that this stress has long afflicted the black colleges, but that it is a substantial problem in all sectors to some extent.

Finally, "income tapering" describes erosion in the real income of colleges. No sector has been able to avoid this effect, although it derives from different sources and is felt more severely in some places than in others. Balderston points out the varying roots of income tapering; universities, for example, lose research funds while gifts to private colleges fail to keep pace with inflation.

Thus, two forces interact to produce exigency: external economic factors beyond control, and internal management that (however organized) decides upon distribution and use of available resources.

Impact of Financial Exigency

Change is impelled by exigency, and most observers seem to agree that higher education will adapt to the conditions it faces. These changes will affect the goals, values, structures, governance processes, and substance of the academic enterprise. The shape of change will depend very much upon whether the response to crisis is in the form of passive adaptation or active constructive grappling with circumstance. Any prediction must assume that conditions will have an impact, not linearly, but differentially across the universe of higher education. Problems will affect differently situated institutions in varying ways, and their responses will partially determine the course and rate of qualitative change.

It is possible, therefore, to foresee myriad outcomes from the same conditions—some positive, some negative—all depending upon how institutions and their managers respond. At present, major dislocations seem unlikely in spite of the ominous portents and the history of sharp discontinuities in the course of higher education in America. Perhaps the only possible predictions at present are those that focus on the evolution of current trends as we know them and as we can anticipate their modification by special institutional considerations.

Mission and Objectives

Institutions vary widely in the goals they pursue. Some have a relatively unitary and strongly supported sense of where they are bound. In theory, crisis can strengthen the vision and commitments of such institutions. Alternatives are more clearly evaluated when matched against defined priorities. These kinds of institutions are, however, particularly vulnerable to cultural and marketplace changes. Will single-sex colleges survive as sex roles merge? Will pure disciplinary research be sustained at a level that permits heavy commitments to graduate education?

Other institutions, perhaps the majority, pursue multiple goals simultaneously, as reflected in the Jencks-Riesman theory of an academic revolution which finds all institutions become increasingly alike in pursuit of the same pantheon of academic values.[9] For these institutions, internal conflict may become more intense as resources grow scarce. Decisions to cut programs or faculty will spark serious intramural dispute, even though the institution itself remains secure in its overall position in the marketplace.

So both increased internal cohesion and increased internal division may result from exigency. By the same reasoning it is evident that some institutions will have to rethink their very purposes, while others will have to adapt by managing conflict. Visionary leaders will do well in some places, but mediators will make better heads elsewhere.

Academic Values

The values of the academic profession, so painstakingly articulated and institutionalized during the past sixty years by the American Association of University Professors, will be under severe pressure as material concerns overpower them. Walter Metzger's eloquent essay on the academic profession in "hard times" predicts the erosion of its normative and spiritual integrity under the abrasive oppression of cost cutting and other forces.[10] To recapitulate his points, a prime issue in the attacks on the profession focuses on the value of academic production as well as on the rate of academic productivity. The latter issue may be resolved with legislated work loads (and has been in Florida), but at bottom is an increasing skepticism about what a professor actually contributes and how its value is to be measured. Presumably, since other voices clamoring for a share of the purse can at least show a more visible—and perhaps unified—claim, the professoriate begins to lose ground economically. Economic weakness accompanies creeping anomie. Metzger argues that rapid expansion of the professoriate and the proliferation of less than fully professional roles in academia during recent years has impaired "professional acculturation" processes and broken the "sense of collegiality" that used to unify a national academic community. The move to unionization and the ascendance of managerial powers, he suggests, may reinforce this loss of professional morale. To what end? Such a radical transformation of professional self-image may result in the loss to society of its trustees of "rationalistic values." The fiduciary quality of faculty performance may disappear behind negotiated contracts and a civil service mentality.

Structural Change

Structural change in the distribution of power and authority will reinforce the trends Metzger has identified as already under way. The Carnegie Foundation senses these winds of change, summarizing their likely result: "One overriding theme is more 'administrative muscle' to shift resources and make better use of them.... The process of decision-making is less academic."[11] In a similar vein, Committee Z of the AAUP foresees that "faculty control over programs and curricula may decline under pressure, to the extent that the influence of students, administrations and governments increase."[12]

As management rights expand, so will the rationality of decision making shift. Academic and professional concerns will be supplanted by a focus on efficiency, productivity, and marketability. Where change in academic institutions has historically paralleled the development of knowledge, it will tend increasingly to follow parochial, political, and economic pressures. Anderson has looked ahead to the consequences of redistributed power and fears for the central value structure of the university.[13] Mainly, he suggests, the increasingly secular involvement in fundamental decisions will reflect the fact that few understand or appreciate the essential social and intellectual functions of the university. This result of financial stress will have more impact on the traditional core of university life—the arts and science colleges and the graduate schools—than on the professional schools, the vocational schools, and on those institutions already subject to centralized management.

Increased Political Awareness

An interesting countertrend to hierarchical administration may be developing, though. Financial stress may lead to increasing political activism among those involved in the educational process. Specifically, faculty and students seem to be mobilizing to defend their own interests before legislatures, executive agencies, and the courts. Paradoxically, as centralized coordinating power becomes institutionalized, the pluralistic voices of higher education's many constituents may become increasingly influential. The seeds of strong student lobbies have been laid at both state and federal levels. Faculty organizations have begun to endorse candidates for national office in an affirmative exercise of self-interest. Facilitating this new activism is a trend on the part of government to open all of its decision-making processes to public scrutiny via sunshine laws.

If political activism does not subtly reshuffle the power equation, it will at least lead to harsher questioning of the rationales behind educational decision making. More careful and thoughtful decision making will be required to overcome charges of arbitrariness, and more affirmative rationalization will have to underlie previously discretionary commitments. The key here is not so much that accountability will increase, but that politicized tests over whose standards of reason will prevail must be handled. There is no guarantee that rational planning models or any particular model of decision making will satisfy the politicized review process. The pressure will grow to develop preventive and preemptive strategies that can effectively withstand assault from all sides. Planning, bargaining, and legal maneuvering will be essential components of these strategies and so will become increasingly valuable skills in educational management.

Innovation and Change

Finally, exigency will require important changes in the process of education. Finding less expensive and more effective ways of accomplishing the university's business will require a close look at the whole "production" process. While economies of institutional operation can be effected in a variety of ways, mostly by trimming overhead, the most promising long-term approach lies in increased productivity. Leslie and Miller used Schumpeter's model of transverse progression to suggest ways of accomplishing this:

1. Introduce new or better products.
2. Alter methods to save labor costs.
3. Find new markets.
4. Find new resources.
5. Reorganize the "industry" via consortia and new distributions of function among institutions.[14]

They detected moves by colleges to adapt in each of these ways as the financial future began to dim in the early 1970s.

These impacts of financial stress do not account for the intense personal effects that will attenuate careers, erode standards of living, contaminate the intrinsic satisfactions of academic work, and otherwise oppress individuals who choose the academic calling. The turning of the economic screw is going to hurt people as well as programs, and the compassion with which they are handled will tell a great deal about where we are headed as a community.

Facing the Future

To say that the future is uncertain is neither original nor helpful. Yet it is an unhappily valid truism. Disparate predictions cloud one's vision of where we are headed and what we can do about it. Howard Bowen, a distinguished and perceptive observer, is bullish on the prospects for a vigorous and effective higher education enterprise. He questions the linear mentality that predicts an oversupply of educated manpower and argues for a new vision of society based squarely on "full development of human capacities."[15] The role of all higher education institutions in such a service-oriented society would be central and its value among institutions paramount. From Bowen's perspective, a reconceived and reinvigorated sense of purpose, thrust, and value would overcome the current and projected doldrums.

Lyman Glenny views the impact of current trends as having differential effects on various sectors of the higher education universe: "The major trends with which we must be concerned in the immediate and distant future will have profound influence on the whole system of postsecondary education, severely crippling the aspirations of some faculties and administrations, and supporting strongly the roles of some institutions and some cadres of teachers long looked upon as being outside the true realm of higher education."[16]

These two views are somewhat more optimistic than those of representatives of more vested interests. John Silber, for example, speaks with particular concern for the future of the "independent" sector, and the AAUP envisions straitened conditions for faculty. So, evidently, predicting for the future has a great deal to do with the catholicity of one's point of view. The larger view recognizes the basic security of the enterprise in a vital, knowledge-based economy, while acknowledging the likelihood of adjustment and change along several dimensions. The narrower view sees severe dislocations for specific sectors and interests. Both seem essentially correct. American society, in its own uncertain future, cannot do without higher education, but it can probably do better *given limited resources* with some changes in the system. Sensing this, in however indirect and inarticulate a fashion, the people can be expected to redirect their investment in education for the purpose of reshaping the mix of returns they get.

Therein lies the opportunity for the academy. By increasing and focusing the *leverage* of society's investment in higher education, we can expect to see our stock rise in value. Investment being largely a matter of faith and confidence, purpose and performance will essentially determine the future level of support for higher education. Although it is a central social institution, the university cannot expect unquestioned legitimacy and support in a time of moral and economic crisis. In the current atmosphere, the academy is not so much a captive of linear trends in population, tax revenues, or other quantitative indices, but of its own atrophied sense of where it is heading and how it might get there. It is toward clearer purpose and more responsive performance that the management of the exigent institution must be directed, for in the end its support will depend on nothing more than how well it does its job—namely, creating, transmitting, and applying knowledge for use in securing and improving the human condition in the universe. The future is secure on only two counts. The fiber of the academy will undergo challenging tests of its strength and flexibility. And its salvation must come from within.

References

1. Andrew H. Lupton, John Augenblick, and Joseph Heyison. "The Financial State of Higher Education." *Change*, September 1976, p. 21ff.

2. Earl Cheit. *The New Depression in Higher Education*. New York: McGraw-Hill, 1971.

3. *A.A.U.P. Bloomfield College Chapter v. Bloomfield College*, 346 A 2d 615 (1975).

4. *Brady v. Board of Trustees of Nebraska State Colleges*, 242 N.W. 2d 161 (1976).

5. Brief *Amicus Curiae* of the American Association of University Professors in Support of Plaintiff-Appellant. *Lumpert v. University of Dubuque*, Case No. 2-57568, Supreme Court of Iowa, May, 1975, p. 17.

6. Ibid., p. 29.

7. James L. Petersen. "The Dismissal of Tenured Faculty for Reasons of Financial Exigency." *Indiana Law Journal*, 51: 417-432, 1976.

8. Frederick E. Balderston. *Managing Today's University*. San Francisco: Jossey-Bass, 1975, pp. 178-198.

9. Christopher Jencks and David Riesman. *The Academic Revolution*. Garden City, New York: Doubleday & Co., 1968.

10. Walter P. Metzger. "The American Academic Profession in 'Hard Times.' " *Daedalus*. 104: 25-44, 1975.

11. Carnegie Foundation for the Advancement of Teaching. *More Than Survival*. San Francisco: Jossey-Bass; 1975, pp. 6-7.

12. Nearly Keeping Up: Report on the Economic Status of the Profession, 1975-76. *AAUP Bulletin*, 62: 195-284, 1976, p. 206.

13. G. Lester Anderson. Governance and Institutional Values: What is at Stake? In *Governance and Emerging Values in Higher Education* (Report No. 12). University Park, Pa: Center for the Study of Higher Education, the Pennsylvania State University, 1971.

14. Larry L. Leslie and Howard F. Miller, Jr. *Higher Education and the Steady State*. Washington: American Association for Higher Education, 1974.

15. Howard R. Bowen. "Higher Education: A Growth Industry?" *Educational Record*. 55: 147-158, 1974.

16. Lyman A. Glenny. "Pressures on Higher Education." *College and University Journal*. 12: 5-9, 1974, p. 5.

Introduction to Chapter 2

Financial exigency coupled with other forces such as academic collective bargaining and centralization of decision making are unquestionably forcing all educational institutions toward better management. In many institutions, the administrative component has been haphazardly constructed, the result of past rapid growth and proliferating demands. Different administrative styles have characterized the educational establishment: paternalistic, authoritarian, participative, and so on. Some have been effective, others have not. Financial exigency contributes to the rationalization of educational administration across all types of institutions and styles of administration because it forces presidents and boards of trustees to become more conscious of their role in managing human resources with the goal of inducing effective and efficient performance.

In Chapter 2 Stephen Finn and William Proctor emphasize the need for greater administrative control over the linkage between institutional activities and institutional mission. They assert the responsibility of the administrative component, including academic supervisors, to clarify the institutional mission in light of market conditions, establish priorities, and determine the proper utilization of resources for goal achievement. They illustrate how the budgetary process and staffing coordination can be powerful tools to promote goal achievement and operating efficiency. They indicate why staff evaluation is extremely important in the labor-intensive organization and urge administrators to institute a personnel development program. These two authors seek to show what lessons educational administrators can learn from their counterparts in the world of business. Because this chapter concentrates on administrative style and organization, it serves as a good introduction to later chapters which describe particular strategies useful in meeting the challenges financial exigency poses.

2

Promoting Management Coordination and Efficiency

Stephen Finn and *William Proctor*

In *The American University*, Jacques Barzun describes colleges and universities as "residual institutions,"[1] attributing to them societal expectations for performing and providing numerous academic and nonacademic services. The expansion of support services in higher education has been particularly phenomenal in America. Placement, counseling, academic advisement, and affirmative action, to name a few, have increased the burden on management and resources. The multiversity is even more reflective of diverse and even non-student-related services such as cooperative extension, hospitals, clinics, home-care programs, specialized research institutes, and continuing education programs.

This expansive involvement has produced three critical consequences at most institutions:

1. Distortion of the institutional mission. (An institution can have many missions, of course, some academic and some service-oriented. For the sake of simplicity, we will simply use the term "mission" to apply to any and all of these purposes in this chapter.)
2. Diminution of the relationship between managerial objectives/activities and overall mission.
3. Inappropriate allocation of resources.

An institution's mission, its managerial objectives and functions, and the allocation of its resources should be intimately interrelated for an educational institution to be operated efficiently. While statements of mission or purpose appear in catalogues and other published documents, they are rarely referred to, reviewed, or updated except for the periodic use of accrediting teams. In fact, the functional mission of many institutions is to become whatever they can become. Internal managerial objectives are nonexistent or bear little relationship to the institutional mission; consequently, institutional resources (personnel, time, money, etc.) become overextended or misdirected. During periods of growth, the importance of the relationship among institutional mission, objectives, and resources is not obvious; however, during periods of no growth and decline, the importance of the relationship becomes critical to the health and survival of the institution.

David Leslie has clearly defined the challenge of financial exigency in the previous chapter. The first part of this chapter creates a framework for the application of management strategies by exploring the critical relationship

19

between institutional mission and the activities of management. In a sense, all the strategies discussed in this book relate in one way or another to the overall mission of the institution. This is not a plea for the adoption of a rigid management-by-objectives approach, but rather a call for a clarification of institutional purpose and a conscious effort to link managerial responsibilites to it. The remainder of the chapter focuses on specific strategies to promote institutional efficiency and effective staff evaluation.

Missions, Objectives, and Managerial Responsibility

Clarifying Mission and Setting Priorities

The importance of establishing a clear institutional mission, especially in the face of a fiscal crisis, can be described through a case study. We have selected a private institution because private higher education has had to face financial exigency earlier than most public institutions. For the private institution, adjusting to hard times can be a particularly traumatic experience, since institutional survival may very well be at stake.

An examination of the developments at New York University over the past twenty years explicitly highlights the critical relationships mentioned above. As J. Victor Baldridge details in his book *Power and Conflict in the University*, New York University was, by decision, a "school of opportunity."[2] Two of the other major universities in New York City—Columbia University and City University— had rigorous admissions standards and, as such, were considered legitimate members of the elite eastern higher education establishment. This left an identifiable void in New York City which was filled by New York University.

From its inception, New York University offered academically disadvan- taged students the chance to obtain quality postsecondary education. During the late 1950s and early 1960s only about 18 percent of the approximate 2300 entering freshmen had SAT scores above 600. A 1956 self-study report predicted increased enrollments for New York University from 1956 through 1966; however, by 1962 enrollment had decreased and it became evident that expected enrollments would not be realized, largely because of the expansion of both the State University and City University of New York.

Partly by circumstance and partly by design, NYU had the good manage- ment sense to develop a plan of action. The steps New York University took during this period very possibly prevented its total collapse. In 1962, under the guidance of its new president Dr. James Hester, New York University began to reevaluate its educational mission. The result was the articulation of six institutional goals which would serve as a bedrock for future educational and managerial decisions:

1. The consolidation of the undergraduate colleges.
2. The recruitment of more full-time students.
3. The recruitment of more full-time faculty.
4. The upgrading of undergraduate admission policies.
5. The upgrading of graduate and professional programs.
6. The concentration on urban affairs and urban service.

As at NYU, statements about institutional mission must be defined in terms sufficiently specific to permit the derivation of operational objectives. It is then necessary to assign operative priorities for each objective. The designation of priorities depends on comprehensive long-range planning in the sense that long-range planning permits an analysis of the implications of proposed objectives, thereby affording a basis for establishing the relative merits of each. Numerous questions must be asked. For example, what objectives must be achieved to ensure the continuing existence of the institution? What objectives are necessary to promote and define institutional growth and/or progress? What objectives are so important that the administration is willing to incur a short-term operating deficit or reallocation of funds to accomplish them? What objectives can be altered or eliminated to achieve those of higher priority? In summary, *the establishment of programmatic priorities lends clarity and structure to the activities and related administrative functions to be performed within an institution.*

Administrative Responsibilities

The impetus and authority for defining the overall institutional mission and guiding the development of specific objectives should obviously originate at the highest level of the institution, the president's office. A piecemeal approach involving separate components of the institution is almost surely doomed to failure from the start, resulting only in an increasing waste of resources. The situation at New York University reflects the importance of the relationship between mission/objectives and managerial functions. As a result of reevaluating its educational mission, NYU made a concerted effort to upgrade its undergraduate admission standards. From 1963 to 1967 the university denied admission to a large number of applicants who most likely would have been offered admission prior to 1963; consequently, freshmen enrollment decreased by as much as 20 percent. However, the percentage of entering freshmen with SAT scores over 600 increased by over 33 percent during this period. By 1968 freshmen enrollment had returned to the level of the pre-1963 era. The initiative and pressure to achieve the upgrading came from top administrative officials during these years.

Management must creatively and industriously direct the energies and resources of the institution towards realizing established objectives. As part of this process, it would be helpful for top-level management to require each academic and nonacademic unit within the organization to define its operating objectives in relation to the overall institutional mission and to recommend allocation of its resources in relation to these objectives. Furthermore, each unit should also be required to develop means of assessing progress toward meeting these objectives and to submit periodic reports indicating how corresponding activities relate to the realization of objectives. It is of paramount importance that this periodic reporting not become a ritual but rather an opportunity for administrators and those for whom they are responsible to develop means of enhancing the potential for effectively serving the overall mission of the institution. Units not meeting this end should be assisted in revising their objectives and activities or be phased out if the revision is not worth the cost.

Every institution should have a timeline calendar for establishing and refining the objectives of each unit, as well as for their assessment and evaluation. As a continuous process, the development and refinement of objectives will assure that each component of the institution relates to overall institutional goals, even if those goals change from time to time in the face of altered circumstances.

When resources are improperly allocated, chance for conflict between mission and objectives is increased. An example of ineffectual managerial coordination among mission, objectives, and resource allocation becomes evident when reviewing budget levels and allocations at small private colleges during the past few years. From 1971 to 1973 many institutions experienced enrollment declines while total operating expenditures increased. Furthermore, a recent study showed that while 17 percent of those institutions surveyed reported losses of FTE enrollment of 10 percent or more, only 14 percent reported upwards of a 5 percent decrease in faculty.[3] While not a direct relationship, the trend is clear. Projections for the future are not encouraging. From 1974 through 1980 enrollments are expected to decline; yet a majority of presidents indicated in the same survey that they expected little change in the number of faculty at their institution over the same period.[4] This is an apparent statistical example of administrative reluctance and faculty refusal to react constructively to financial exigency. Since salaries constitute 60 to 85 percent of most educational budgets, only through attrition or retrenchment of personnel and programs or a reallocation of these resources can institutions, public or private, be saved. Cutbacks in supplies and maintenance operations are stopgap measures at best. As a matter of fact, repeated cuts in maintenance operations have proven to *increase* costs later on. Postponed maintenance and rehabilitation of plant and equipment are hardly tributes to effective management. It is essential that institutional missions be redefined and that organizational components be forced to realign their objectives and programs with overall goals if institutional mediocrity or even demise is to be prevented. In a sense, what we are suggesting is an application of the zero-base budgeting approach to the programmatic activities of educational institutions, at least on a periodic basis. Failure to approach the challenge of financial exigency rationally *before* a crisis develops will leave little alternative to rapid retrenchment, a last-ditch strategy explored in greater detail in Chapter 5.

Proper utilization of resources requires that every decision to expand or contract programs, to add or decrease academic or nonacademic personnel, and to build or close physical facilities be evaluated for its long-term institutional implications. Decisions requiring the long-term commitment of resources that are made in the absence of competent analysis of markets, finances, and program and personnel options preclude long-term institutional stability. Many institutions have been haphazard in their projection of costs for new programs or personnel beyond initial start-up costs.

In general, and particularly during periods of financial exigency, the focus of responsibility firmly rests with management for coordinating the allocation of resources with institutional objectives and for monitoring and adjusting to the impact of external pressure on the institution. Strong executive organization and control will result in progressive leadership which can provide:

1. Clarity on the part of major and intermediate administrators regarding their authority and responsibilities. Effective personnel evaluation will only occur when objectives are clearly identified and supervisory responsibility in fulfilling objectives is identified.
2. Strong evidence of effective long-range planning. Long-range planning manifests itself in consistency of direction toward mutual goals. Further, so-called master plans constructed to satisfy the demands of trustees or centralized agencies will be more directly related to actual institutional functioning. Planned commitments to future change will hasten institutional vitality.
3. Greater self-satisfaction on the part of managerial staffers. This manifests itself in long-term commitment by innovative and goal-oriented administrators and an atmosphere of higher morale. The alternative is a staff that mutes its concerns and input, and retreats to the false security of doing nothing.
4. Sharpened ability to respond to external demands and requests. This manifests itself in various ways from increased funds and grants to more favorable agency audits.
5. Executive support for lower level administrative actions. This manifests itself in the effective decision making that cooperation and mutual respect always bring about.
6. Increased ability to monitor and plan for external changes. This manifests itself by a more constructive approach to impending crises and by greater ability to cope successfully with actual crises if they should occur.

Strategies to Promote Goal Achievement and Efficiency

The Budgetary Process

Since resource commitment is essential to goal achievement, the budgetary process takes on renewed importance in the institution faced with adjusting to times of financial exigency. Simply stated, if used correctly the budgetary process is a most important managerial tool. If used incorrectly, the budgetary process is a time-consuming and costly diversion from important institutional needs.

The budget must be prepared at the academic and administrative level and fully understood by those involved. For too long budgets and budgetary categories have annually increased or decreased on an across-the-board basis, with little, if any, recognition of objectives and priorities. At all times, but particularly during times of financial exigency, the budget must reflect managerial objectives and priorities. Periodic workshops should be arranged to train key administrators in the budgetary process and its relationship to the accomplishment of the mission and objectives of the institution. Many key administrators are promoted from the academic ranks, where their attention to academic concerns may have prohibited them from gaining the skills necessary to devise and administer budgets. Conversely, the budgetary experts must forego their territorial concerns to provide those unversed in the process with both training and information.

As an aid to determining final accountability, each department might well submit a periodic written statement (in nonfinancial language) of actual expenditures and their relationship to prescribed objectives and priorities. It is very likely that projected expenditures and actual expenditures will be at variance because of unforeseen circumstances. The budget, and those responsible for its implementation, must be flexible and adjust to these changes according to preplanned procedures. A gradual move towards zero-base budgeting might also help clarify objectives and priorities. In fact, in an era of fiscal stringency, periodic imposition of zero-base budgeting techniques may be preferable to more popular incremental budgeting. By requiring total justification for planned expenditures, an additional tool for assessing objectives is acquired. This does not have to be accomplished each year, but may be scheduled at intervals appropriate to the character of the institution.

A review of the year-end financial statements should serve as a starting point for developing next year's budget. The reasons for and implications of prior-year budget shifts should be analyzed. It is imperative that administrators understand the relationship between long-term capital or personnel investments and the future allocation of resources. For example, during the past ten years many colleges and universities secured sophisticated computer systems without a competent assessment of institutional needs. It soon became evident that many of these institutions did not have the managerial research or reporting needs to warrant such systems, but once the initial decision was acted upon, the institution tacitly committed substantial amounts of money to equipment and specialized personnel. Ego will too often prevent the removal of wasteful programs once they become institutionalized.

At all times, programmatic and personnel decisions must be made only after careful consideration of their impact on institutional objectives, resource allocation, and managerial activity. Before reaching a decision regarding a proposed action, an administrator must review the following concerns:

1. In what way(s) will the proposed action assist the realization of our institutional mission and objectives?
2. What are the alternate methods of achieving this proposed action?
3. If we take this action, what is the total short- or long-term commitment of institutional resources?

The merit of this approach is not limited to private institutions. While current economic circumstances may contribute to the difficulties now confronted by state systems of higher education, a fair evaluation might suggest that the missions of many of these systems are ill defined, lacking in specificity, or remotely related to administrative activities.

Staff Utilization and Coordination

After priorities have been specified, it is necessary to delegate responsibility for accomplishing the objectives. Responsibility should be delegated to administrative officers rather than to administrative units or committees. Committees should be limited to consultation and recommending functions since they cannot realistically be responsible for their actions. Administrative functions may be described in terms of particular activities, but the responsibility for achieving specific objectives must reside with the administrative officers and those they supervise. This enables responsibility to be pinpointed in later evaluation sessions. In this connection, department chairpersons must be considered administrative officers with the same first-line responsibilities as supervisors of nonfaculty employee groups. Academic departments, in turn, must be considered subunits of the institution, each with a set of objectives to accomplish in relation to the overall institutional mission. Where department chairpersons are ineffective by tradition or by inclusion in a bargaining unit with teaching faculty, top-level administrators may have to develop a new layer of front-line administrators capable of exerting effective management responsibility.

It is axiomatic that the most significant objectives will necessitate supporting efforts from the divisions of an institution. However, the recognition of this requirement should not result in the diffusion of responsibility to the extent that accountability is rendered meaningless. To preclude such diffusion, the administrator responsible for achieving a particular objective must identify the necessary supporting activities, delegate specific responsibility for providing the necessary service to the appropriate administrative officers, and make sure that these supporting functions are consistent with the priority of the major objective from which these functions are derived. This will require a close and continuous evaluative process.

It is futile for an administrator to endeavor to accomplish an objective of high priority when the related supporting functions are relegated to secondary importance. Moreover, it is unlikely that a member of an administrative staff can personally exert the authority necessary to ensure that supporting activities are properly considered by other administrators of equal rank. The president must act to ensure that the overall institutional mission is realistic and specific, must require the appropriate derivation of operational objectives, must delegate these objectives to other administrators of the institution, and must insist upon appropriate administrative attention to all related supporting functions. The president alone has the power to ensure cooperation. Once his or her position is made clear, then key administrators can work cooperatively with those they supervise to achieve direction in their respective units by developing job descriptions and related evaluation devices.

The specification of priorities makes possible the resolution of competing claims for resources. Priorities provide the basis upon which the institutional budget is aligned with institutional objectives. Priorities determine which programs are added, expanded, revised, curtailed, or eliminated. When one considers the personnel actions related to program adjustments, the significance of priorities is even more apparent, especially during times of financial stress.

A single example may suffice to illustrate these points. Assume that an institution has designated the recruitment of a superior faculty as an operational objective and has assigned the highest priority to this goal. The basic responsibility for accomplishing this objective is delegated appropriately to the chief academic officer. However, there are several key supporting tasks. For a private institution, and increasingly for public institutions as well, the director of development must make certain that fund-raising activities are designed to provide support for faculty research, library acquisitions, etc. Since soliciting funds is easier when donor interest is directed toward capital improvements, the understanding and support of the director of development is essential. Unfortunately, fund-raising activities are often only remotely related to the prescribed priorities of the institution.

Likewise, the administrator responsible for the budget must act to ensure that the operating budget is developed to facilitate the efforts of the chief academic officer in securing a superior faculty. The budget director must be alert to opportunities to divert funds to the support of faculty recruitment. Such opportunities are not always self-evident, and it is unlikely that they will be identified unless the faculty recruitment program is assigned a high priority within the office responsible for the budget.

The director of admissions should make certain that prospective students are aware of the new objective and its relevance to their needs, as well as to the fact that certain programs or activities may have to be curtailed to ensure a superior faculty. Increasingly, admissions officers are taking on the characteristics of marketing personnel in the industrial sector as they endeavor to articulate how their college's programs provide valuable services worth the cost to the student. Effective communication to prospective clients entails an intimate awareness of institutional objectives and their priorities. As Eugene Fram, Director of the Center for Management Study at the Rochester Institute of Technology, points out, "Through marketing, the college or university develops the philosophy that institutional success is the result of solving long and short range problems for all types of clients."[5]

Similarly, the office of student services must support the effort by candidly responding to student inquiries or complaints concerning allocation of institutional resources. Student services personnel cannot adopt a passive or defensive attitude regarding the high priority assigned to the objective. They must promote student understanding and ultimately student pride in the importance of the faculty recruitment program and provide important feedback to higher level administrators.

The desired quality of administrative support presupposes a strong sense of unity and commitment regarding the mission and objectives of the institution. For years administrators and faculty have undertaken the costly and time-consuming ritual of self-evaluation, five-year plans, and institutional assessments, only to continue to operate on a "business as usual basis." *In the final analysis, the translation of institutional missions and objectives into functional activities will determine the future of the institution.* The responsibility for the translation of missions and objectives into effective organizational activity squarely rests with top-level management, most importantly with the president. Not only must initiative for meaningful change start there, but also the coordination of staff and resources to implement new goals must emanate from the highest management levels.

Staff Evaluation and Accountability

Only through competent performance review and evaluation can staff members be effective and beneficial to the institution.[6] Specifically, performance review is critical for three reasons:

1. It provides a basis for the assessment of progress towards goal realization.
2. It provides a basis for the assessment of personnel.
3. It provides a basis for the assessment for future planning needs.

Notwithstanding an appreciation of the need for performance review, college and university administrators confront major problems in developing and implementing workable review procedures for use within higher education. One reason that problems develop is that procedures for performance review have been developed for use within the business sector and, as such, are strictly related to objectives, outputs, and profits. Many colleges and universities, in an attempt to review performance, have utilized the business technique of "management by objectives" (MBO) only to discover that the identification and measurement of outcomes associated with specific objectives are not always obvious in higher education. Recent reports, however, seem to indicate that attempts to measure heretofore relatively unmeasured activity are on the increase.

From a managerial perspective many organizational elements present within the business sector are not reflected within higher education. Any attempt to strictly apply business concepts and techniques to the management of higher education without adjusting for the different organizational structures will not produce the desired results.

Succinctly stated, the two aspects of higher education usually considered to make the development and implementation of effective review performance difficult are intangible and diverse objectives and immeasurable outputs. In his paper, *An Approach to Planning and Management Systems Implementation*, James Farmer notes that higher education is a complex process that contributes to the individual, to society, and to business. Its product is the result of integrating inputs such as classroom instruction, laboratory periods, libraries, and so on in a complex, largely immeasurable way.[7]

The relationship among goals, objectives, outputs, and performance review is inseparable. Therefore if educational institutions are to become financially stable, administrators must develop and implement a managerial system that integrates these elements within the unique organizational structures of the educational organization.

We have already described administrative responsibility for clarifying mission and objectives. We have noted administrative responsibility for assigning priorities to objectives, providing adequate funds for their achievement, and coordinating staffing in light of the hierarchy of organizational or subunit goals. But performing these tasks and ignoring evaluation is like clapping with one hand. How can we be sure that our staffing arrangements are adequate to achieving assigned objectives? What can we do to remedy deficiencies in both staffing patterns and personnel effectiveness? Clearly, *performance review* is a most critical managerial responsibility. And we cannot hide behind the "goal diffuse" nature of the educational institution to evade responsibility for its implementation.[8]

It is the responsibility of key administrators to evaluate job performance and act upon unsatisfactory activity. This is as true for the nonteaching staff as it is for the faculty. Individuals whose performances are below expectation must be retrained or replaced. A critical component of any evaluation system is the *remedial program*. How are staff members to acquire new information, insight, skills? While a personnel development program is beyond the scope of this chapter, we can emphasize its importance here, particularly in light of the fiscal, legal, and humanitarian obstacles to dismissing staff members. It may be more efficient in the long run to reassign or retrain existing staff members than to retrench them. Many materials currently on the market or in stages of construction describe the elements of a personnel evaluation and development program, and we strongly urge administrators to explore them.[9] In any case, staff development and retraining should become an ongoing process, one integrated into the system.

Before we can benefit from the diagnostic character of an evaluation system, it is essential that objectives be established for each employee in each subunit of the institution in light of the overall functioning of that unit. It is also vitally important that *evaluative criteria* be developed which are related to the objectives and a periodic *evaluation process* be constructed. How is this to be done in an organization as complex and multifaceted as the educational institution? Some staff evaluation systems can be developed centrally, for example, those relating to high-level administrators, including deans, vice presidents, and their staffs. But in other situations, it is probably preferable for subunits to develop their own evaluation systems. Thus, the personnel evaluation system for payroll and purchasing will be considerably different from the system in an academic department or the counseling office.

Of course, institutional, state, or contractual arrangements may limit options. But in any case, we believe *it is important that an evaluation occur and the results be utilized to improve staff performance*. Not only is this the best way to promote efficiency in a labor-intensive industry such as higher education, it is probably the most effective way to promote job satisfaction and high morale.

Summary

In this chapter we have tried to impress upon educational administrators the lessons they can learn from their counterparts in the industrial sector. We acknowledge that solutions to problems facing higher education do not lie in the strict application of business techniques to educational operations. Institutions of higher education are people-processing organizations, highly labor-intensive, characterized by a relatively low level of technology, and committed to a variety of goals.

Nevertheless, educational administrators will be making a grave mistake to let these characteristics blind them to the application of business techniques that can help rationalize organizational operation and promote operating efficiency. It simply no longer makes good sense to operate on a "business as usual" basis. We believe administrators must assume responsibility for defining the overall mission of their institution, promoting the development of specific objectives in light of the mission, establishing priorities for achieving these objectives, and providing adequate funds and staffing patterns to assure implementation. Critically important to the success of this approach in a labor-intensive industry is the establishment of an effective system of staff evaluation and development.

References

1. Jacques Barzun. *The American University: How It Runs, Where It is Going*. New York: Harper and Row, 1968, p. 10.

2. J. Victor Baldridge. *Power and Conflict in the University*. New York: John Wiley, 1971, p. 39.

3. Lyman Glenny, John Shea, Janet Ruyle, and Kathryn Freschi. *Presidents Confront Reality: From Edifice Complex to University Without Walls*. San Francisco: Jossey-Bass, 1976, p. 35.

4. Ibid., p. 33.

5. Eugene H. Fram. "Organizing the Marketing Focus in Higher Education." Paper presented at the Annual Forum of the Association for Institutional Research, May 1975, p. 2.

6. Peter Drucker. *Management: Tasks, Responsibilities, Practices.* New York: Harper and Row, 1974.

7. James Farmer. *An Approach to Planning and Management Systems Implementation.* Monograph for the California State University and College System, 1971, pp. 2-3.

8. For helpful information about evaluation concepts and techniques, see Scarvia B. Anderson, Samuel Ball, and Richard T. Murphy. *Encyclopedia of Educational Evaluation*. San Francisco: Jossey-Bass, 1974. See also Paul L. Dressel, *Handbook of Academic Evaluation*. San Francisco: Jossey-Bass, 1976.

9. See, for example, the bibliography in *Faculty Development in a Time of Retrenchment*, a monograph by *Change* Magazine, 1974. See also the bibliographies at the end of various sections in Sally S. Gaff, Conrad Festa, and Jerry G. Gaff, *Resource Notebook*, published by the Project on Institutional Renewal. This publication can be purchased for a nominal sum by writing 1818 R. Street, N.W., Washington, D.C. 20009.

Introduction to Chapter 3

The current fiscal crisis in higher education has heightened the demand for data, accountability, and better management. William Collard, James Farmer, and John Harrison explain why systems analysis can help respond to these demands. Speaking not to the expert but to the generalist administrator in both secondary and higher education, the authors discuss the variety of system models currently available. They avoid proselytizing about the subject, pointing out the limitations of the systems approach and the high cost involved. More importantly, they acknowledge that various types of institutions can benefit from some models, but not from others. And they offer specific examples.

After providing a comprehensive definition of planning and management systems, Collard, Farmer, and Harrison trace the development of systems analysis as a response to demands that higher education be better managed. They describe descriptive systems, predictive systems, and resource models, and they provide a variety of illustrations. Campus-based administrators will find their discussion of potential outcomes and the implementation processes particularly helpful.

The authors have extensive professional training and experience in the implementation, application, and evaluation of planning and management systems. All are experienced consultants and authors in this highly technical field.

3

The Systems Approach to Educational Management

William J. Collard, James Farmer,
and *John G. Harrison*

Our educational system includes a wide variety of educational institutions with ever-changing missions, objectives, and procedures. Their differences may be obvious or subtle. Change may be rapid or slow. While the institutions and the education processes associated with them may be viewed in different ways, one method of viewing them is the systems approach—a simple, but powerful, conceptual view.

The systems approach to decision making does not always require a highly sophisticated approach, computer models, data bases, or statistical analysis. Rather, the systems approach can be a more simplified manual method, but still requiring specific goals that can be translated into measurable objectives, alternatives expressed in quantitative terms, and an evaluation of these alternatives in relation to the objectives. However, educational institutions are so complex that the data needed to describe education processes, in even the most simplistic form, become extensive. Thus, the representation of educational processes usually requires computer models or statistical analysis. That is, the systems approach to planning and management in educational institutions in practice is implemented through data systems, computer models, statistical packages, and query languages. Because most of these mechanisms are also called systems, the term "planning and management systems" is used to distinguish these "tools" from other kinds of systems, such as computer operational systems, management information systems, and so on.

The systems approach views an educational program as having students enrolled in a program of instruction. The outcome of that program is a student with some increment in education. The inputs to the process are faculty, counselors, instructional materials, facilities, and support. Unlike a production process which produces a tangible product, there is no one "optimum mix" of these inputs that produces an educational output. There are many different methods of instruction. Some programs use instructional materials heavily, others use none. The institutional environment may affect the outcomes significantly. In primary and secondary education where educational objectives have been defined more specifically over a longer period of time, there is no general agreement on what produces the effectiveness or quality of education. Yet, in spite of these major complexities, the systems approach has contributed to improved planning and management of institutions. As one "tool" an educational administrator may use, the systems approach is bringing an additional perspective to the particular problems posed by the financial exigencies of today's "new environment."

33

Development and Implementation of Planning and Management Systems

The Development Phase

Although the concepts and early experimental work in planning and management systems began in the 1930s, the combination of new technology, institutional affluence, foundation and federal government support, and potential competition for funds gave rise to both institutional and national projects for developing planning and management systems in the 1960s and 1970s. The primary and secondary schools were deeply involved in program budgeting, either voluntarily or through state-level coercion. The higher education institutions were responding to state pressures or the opportunities presented by the National Center for Higher Education Management Systems (NCHEMS), a national project then, focusing on institutional decision making. By the early 1970s, the pressures for more sophisticated planning and management had become intense. There were increasingly major shortages of funds at all levels. Federal, state, and local government increased reporting requirements and program justifications based on extensive data analysis. Internally, programmatic and personnel planning increasingly demanded comprehensive cost accounting, since major decisions about these matters are very likely to be heavily influenced by budgetary considerations.

As a result of the demands, a number of models and computer-based data collection and reporting systems were developed. Most of these tools for systems analysis in education followed the availability of inexpensive computing—about 1964 with the third generation of computers—and ended in the mid 1970s when the focus shifted to policy analysis at the state and federal levels. Policy analysis is a specialized and more sophisticated form of systems analysis. Almost all the planning and management systems used today at the institutional level were developed between 1964 and 1974.

Incentive for Implementation

Although most of the development activities have ceased, institutions, districts, and governing boards continue to implement planning and management systems. These systems are now being used for four reasons.

First, manual records and limited clerical and research staff are no longer adequate for responding to the many requests from internal and external agents for information, analysis, and justification; some automation is necessary. While most institutions had accepted the annual budget cycle, in 1975 and 1976 New York City did not hesitate to ask the City University of New York (CUNY) to completely rebudget the next year in one or two days. The entire planning process had to be compressed into this available time. CUNY colleges and universities such as Kingsborough Community College that had automated planning systems were able to identify the impact of new financial constraints and respond with programmatic changes. The remaining institutions had no choice but to administer uniform budget reductions. The assumption is, of course, that institutions with automated systems were able to respond more rationally than those without this capability. Only future study of CUNY decision making during this period will tell the final story. We believe, however, that if information is to have any value or use in decision making, it must be available before the decision is made.

This criterion—timeliness—has motivated many institutions to install planning and management systems and to use the systems approach. Because of the fiscal pressures institutions are experiencing, it is not possible either to reduce the budget incrementally or to survive on small increases without threatening academic quality. Thus these planning tools become particularly useful when major program changes must occur or when special revenue increasing efforts are required. But perhaps the most important contribution has been to identify the future results of current actions and events so that institutional management can carefully evaluate alternatives before events render them impractical or unfeasible. In fact, the most widespread use of these models has been the analysis of historical data as part of an effort to control expenditures. Direct program and discipline costs are examined to identify low utilization of facilities and faculty, the enrollment data is used to identify low or decreasing program of course enrollments, and the general financial models are used to compare administrative and other support costs between institutions. All these data are used to identify areas for more specific investigation and, in conjunction with careful judgment, to suggest corrective actions.

Second, perhaps the most useful result of the systems approach has been the collection of increased data about the educational process itself. One of the early activities of the National Center for Higher Education Management Systems (NCHEMS) was training in the use of a "resource prediction model." The first model, MICRO-U, had only three student majors (programs) and three departments.[1] But it was used extensively by teams during training sessions. From these exercises and similar training in the systems approach, the participants were able to recognize more clearly the complexity and nature of some of the interactions within the institution. While such knowledge can also be obtained through years of experience, this "synthetic" experience provides additional insight that will assist educational administrators as they guide their institutions through the period of financial exigency. For many educational administrators these insights have stimulated new alternatives as the environment and financing of education shifted rapidly. Similarly, the resource analysis underlying most predictive models revealed many relationships that were previously only a matter of speculation. Two excellent examples are the 1974 annual reports of the State

University College at Plattsburgh, New York, and the recent Master Plan of Colorado State University at Greeley.

Third, while educational institutions have always tried to be accountable for "dollars spent," traditional accounting systems are unequal to modern demands. Program budgeting and zero-base budgeting, for example, require extensive data arrayed in several different ways. Lacking any better organization of data, control agencies and governing boards often resort to gross interinstitutional comparisons based on noncomparative data. Many institutions have found that the results of systems analysis have enabled them to better demonstrate accountability and to articulate the specific differences or circumstances of the educational programs at their institutions. At SUNY-Plattsburgh, for example, systems analysis was instrumental in reallocating faculty resources to programs with increasing enrollments even though the total institutional enrollment was in a planned decline.

Fourth, the developers of planning and management systems in education were aware of the political environment in which all these systems were to operate. But they did not foresee one of the most significant uses of the results of systems analysis—a potent weapon for persuasion. Having no other well-defined procedures, trustees, legislators, and executive officers rely on the results—costs, completion rates, enrollments, resource utilization—for their financing formulas, performance measures, and control parameters. This has placed special significance on the financial reporting procedures adopted by the American Institute of Certified Public Accountants, the costing procedures of the National Center for Higher Education Management Systems, and the data reporting conventions of the National Center for Education Statistics in its Elementary and Secondary General Information Survey (ELSEGIS) and Higher Education General Information Survey (HEGIS). Many current financing formulas now use program enrollments, completion rates, tuition response, and historical, program, and marginal costs produced by these various data reporting systems.

Types of Systems

Two major types of planning and management systems, or tools, are used in the systems approach. These are *descriptive systems* and *predictive systems*. The descriptive systems organize and summarize data in an array that provides an institutional overview for the educational administrator. The institution's financial report is one of the simplest descriptive systems. By contrast, the predictive system attempts to identify future conditions based on current data, assumptions about the future, and relationships modeled in the predictive system. It may be useful to review some of the most widely used systems of each type.

Descriptive Systems

Basic descriptive statistics—totals, subtotals by type, averages, number or percentage by class—are essential to all decision makers. The most widely available are the Elementary and Secondary Education General Information Survey (ELSEGIS) and the Higher Education General Information Survey (HEGIS) of the National Center for Education Statistics. Because these data are collected by defined procedures and organized into statistical reports, ELSEGIS and HEGIS can be considered a planning and management system providing descriptive statistics. Several states, following the example of the National Commission on the Financing of Postsecondary Education, have organized these data into machine-readable data bases accessible through query languages and statistical packages (general computer programs used for statistical analysis). Data and associated statistics are available on enrollments, awards, faculty and staff, finances, libraries, and facilities. Almost all institutions contribute to these national surveys as well as to specialized state reports. The ELSEGIS and HEGIS data are available in machine-readable, well-documented form from either the National Center for Education Statistics (NCES) or organizations like the National Education Data Library (NEDL). (Machine-readable means that the data is in a form that can be directly read by a computer, usually punched cards, or magnetic tape. Because of different formats and cost, data is usually not transferred using disks or cassettes.)

A number of analytical tools provide certain descriptive data for determining the resources required for education institutions. One of the most comprehensive systems today is the Costing and Data Management Systems (CADMS). CADMS was developed by NCHEMS primarily for collecting and arraying the data for use in a predictive model—the NCHEMS Resource Requirements Prediction Model (RRPM)-1.6.[2, 3] However, in implementing CADMS,[4] a number of institutions have discovered a variety of other uses for the descriptive data this system provides. The descriptive data provided by CADMS can be classified into three categories:

1. *Student Data*. These data are necessary to describe the resource consuming pattern of the students. In today's language, this student consumption pattern is referred to as an Instructional Workload Matrix (IWLM). An IWLM identifies the relationship between the instructional organizational units (e.g., departments, disciplines, courses) and instructional student programs. Basically, an IWLM can be viewed in two ways. First, the IWLM displays the units (e.g., credit hours, courses, etc.) that each organizational unit contributes to each student program. Second, it displays the units that each student program consumes from each organizational unit. With this matrix, coupled with the dollars expended by each organizational unit, CADMS can calculate and provide the unit cost of each organizational unit and student program. Therefore, the educational administrator can determine the cost of educating one biology major

or the cost to the philosophy department of offering an elective or required course to that same biology major. The educational planner can view costs in several dimensions prior to making programmatic decisions.

2. *Personnel Data.* These data primarily describe how the instructional resources are being used to influence the student behavior pattern, increase student knowledge or skill level, increase student job potential, and so on. Typically, a single institutional financial account supports a varied number of activities such as instruction, research, public service, etc. The personnel data provided to CADMS assist in identifying the resources contributed to each of the activities identified in the analysis. As a result of these data, CADMS provides such descriptive data as faculty rank mix, salary schedules by rank, faculty workload measures and full-time equivalent (FTE) faculty. These data can be readily used by the educational planner to predict future salary costs. Additional data can be added to determine predictive retirement schedules or tenure impact. Salary increases for collective bargaining purposes can be programmed to determine immediate and long-range costs.

3. *Financial Data.* Typically these data describe the way dollar resources for the educational institution were assigned to its organizational units, and how these units expended their dollar resources (salary, wages, supplies, etc.). These data are especially helpful to the educational manager and budget officers who wish to determine if budget requests by function are actually being expended in line with previous justifications.

The Costing and Data Management Systems arrays these three basic types of data and provides an historical analysis of how an institution's resources were actually introduced and used in the educational process. The resulting descriptive data from the CADMS analysis can be used to provide multiple insights useful to the institutional planning and management process. For example, Figure 5-1 displays one department in terms of faculty by type of appointment, salary, sex, and racial group. This simplistic example can be manually completed to provide minimal impact data for the management decision-making process. If the CADMS data were available, however, management could simultaneously evaluate various options for immediate *and* for long-range impact quickly and accurately. This would accommodate both short-term and long-range planning into one phase of retrenchment decision making.

Two of the most important resources in institutions are faculty and facilities. Many states and institutions collected data on these resources. One such example is a descriptive display of faculty and facilities utilization. It provides charts and maps so that patterns of use—by time, by type of facility, by type or department affiliation of the faculty—can be visualized by the education administrator. In addition, the traditional utilization rates or workload are computed according to several different policies and standards.

Predictive Systems and Resource Models

Conceptually the most simple enrollment project model is the student flow model. This concept is simply following students as they advance from one level or program to another according to a statistical pattern. Yet few institutions have implemented a student flow model, and only Nebraska has maintained a student flow model for several years.[5] The usual observation from these models is that a student has a much more complex, though predictable, path through the educational system than originally believed. Many of the results (e.g., more students transfer from universities to community colleges than from community colleges to universities) are either counterintuitive or demythologizing.

A number of models have been designed specifically to predict the amount of classroom space (square footage by type of facility) required for a specified enrollment. The results of these models have led to space formulas of generally accepted standards. One model, however, used the actual enrollments by class and time to determine if remodeling would accommodate the enrollments or indicated the smallest amount of additional space needed to accommodate a particular pattern of use by students. This model could be used for scheduling if facilites were the constraining factors.

A number of educational predictive computer models are presently available to institutions. Probably the most widely used predictive models in higher education are the NCHEMS Resource Requirements Prediction Model, its predecessor the Cost Estimation Model, and commercial derivatives. The NCHEMS model identifies future requirements for staff, budgets, and (in some versions) space, based on current and projected program enrollments, resource ratios, and departmental preferences by program enrollees. One of the most inexpensive and facile to implement and use is the Resource Requirements Prediction Model (RRPM)-1.6 developed by NCHEMS during the early 1970s. In the past, this system has been implemented for costs ranging from $1,550 to $18,200 depending on enrollment level. This model has been successfully implemented and used for planning purposes by a wide variety of different institutions, both in the public and private sectors of education.

The RRPM provides a quick and easy method for educational administrators to view numerous alternatives to their pressing limited resource problems. It allows the administrator to ask "what if" resource questions, such as, what if enrollments decrease 5 percent, or what if the student-faculty ratio changes from 20-1 to 15-1, and so on. These questions and others can be addressed to the model which will provide insights into the complex resource issues in making controlled or uncontrolled decisions. The historical data required for implementing RRPM are (1) induced course load matrix, as shown in Figure 3-1 and (2) faculty workloads, (3) distribution of faculty ranks, and (4) faculty salary schedules.

Academic Departments	Student Majors			
	History Major	English Major	Biology Major	Undecided Major
Chemistry Department	6.1	3.0	3.5	4.2
English Department	4.3	9.5	3.4	3.5
Botany Department	2.6	2.1	5.5	3.9
Physics Department	3.0	1.4	3.6	4.4

Figure 3-1. An Example of an Induced Course Load Matrix (ICLM), Showing the *Average* Number of Credit Hours Taken by Each Type of Student Major from Each Academic Department During Some Time Period.

These data are necessary to provide the model with the historical foundation for making resource predictions. The data required by RRPM are formatted by CADMS. Using the data in this way, administrators will be able to gain some insight into the impact on facilities and faculty workload of a planned increase in the faculty-student ratio from 19-1 to 20-1, for example.

Other relatively simple yet powerful tools are the general planning systems. These generally array enrollment, tuition, and expense data in vertical columns for present and future years. Simple relationships between variables are established and used in computation. For example, tuition may equal a constant multiplied by enrollment. Expenses may be fixed, or fixed plus some increment for each student, or enrollments and expenses can be increased by some inflation factor. These simple models are based primarily on financial data. They have been powerful because they have reduced hours of computation to a few minutes, permitting education administrators to examine a number of alternatives as well as to compute a single plan. The impact of changing enrollments, faculty and staff salary patterns, and tuition can be examined. Not only are the specific results of an alternative available, but after a number of attempts the education administrator gains experience with the concepts underlying the process. These systems include IBM's Planning Systems Generator, PLANTRAN (including the original U.S. Office of Education version), and Budget Planning System.

Perhaps the most complex model, in use by some state agencies, is the tuition response or ACCESS model. This model projects the changes in institutional enrollment in each educational sector resulting from varied changes in tuition levels. This model was first used nationally by the National Commission on the Financing of Postsecondary Education to study the impact on student access of different tuition levels. (See reference 5 for a description of the NCFPS model.) The model was improved by the Illinois Board of Higher Education and used by Illinois and Tennessee to evaluate tuition increases. The results show marked shifts of enrollment between educational sectors as tuition rates are either increased or changed relative to each sector. ACCESS closely models the "market" for education and could be used by an institution to examine the effect of tuition on enrollments in its programs.

Some more complex models have been used primarily in research. The cost of implementation for management purposes may be more expensive than any state or institution could justify. These models can cost up to several million dollars each, but those we have discussed have been marketed successfully at relatively low costs. Administrators should be cautious about implementing any program that will not be cost-effective for their particular institution. Both the cost of the implementation and the maximum, minimum, and expected savings should be estimated before implementing any program.

Results of Predictive Systems Use

Many of the predictive models provide descriptive statistics as an intermediate result. For example, faculty productivity—the number of student credit hours per full-time equivalent faculty member—has become an important intermediate result of using the Resource Requirements Prediction Model (RRPM). This definition of productivity has subsequently been incorporated into law and state standards in some areas. Similarly, the patterns of student flows between levels and programs within an institution and between levels and institutions within a state have been useful in examining institutional performance, although these results are only an intermediate step to a computation of future enrollments. Thus, the intermediate results of predictive models can be used to provide useful descriptive statistics, and if a planning and management tool is being designed, any useful intermediate results should be displayed for the educational administrator. It makes good common sense to exploit the potential of any system one adopts.

The users of resource analysis and predictive resource tools must realize that the data provided has to be augmented to describe comprehensively the relative worth of the instructional activities being examined. When NCHEMS recognized that their tools provided only financial information on activities, they developed a method for collecting instructional outcomes data to help users assess the relative quality or value of competing institutional activities.[6] The outcomes data include vocational or educational plans of students completing a college program (average starting salary, field of work, field of study, and so forth), as well as students' perceptions of the institution's contribution to their development in such areas as knowledge and skills, social and cultural appreciations, etc. These types of data are collected through a survey of students who have completed a program of study. NCHEMS realizes that the collection of program completion data alone is inadequate for evaluating student activities and is currently developing other surveys related to alumni, attrition rates, follow-up studies, and so forth. However, it is important to emphasize that every institution must determine what outcomes it expects to achieve. Salary and employment data for graduating students may be important information for a vocational school, while reports of admission to graduate programs may be an important outcome for a select liberal arts college. Thus, the institution must be careful to ask the right questions if its investment in such assessment systems is to pay off.

Another benefit from the implementation and use of predictive systems is often the creation or modification of a data base. Although any collection of data can be termed a data base, the term "data base" has come to mean a completely documented, computer-readable collection of data. Complete documentation usually means a data element dictionary or data base dictionary that provides name, description, definitions, codes, source, and edit criteria. The most common form is the data base directory that does not include edit criteria and has only limited definitions. Computer-readable statistical data from both NCES and NEDL have data base directories. Usually the data is organized as one data record per institution, department, or person. This permits the data base to be used with a query language. The query language provides the user with the ability to select, display, summarize and perform simple statistical operations or tests on these data. General statistical packages usually require the same single-record format.

The term "data base" has also been extended to require the use of a data base management system. This system, a software supplement to a computer's operation, permits the user to request information by its name or its relationship to other data and the data will be located and retrieved. At present, most data base management systems do not have a companion query language, and most query languages and statistical packages will not operate with a data base management system.

At the state level, the data base is usually a statistical collection of aggregated information about institutions. Like ELSEGIS and HEGIS, the data represents the results obtained from single institutions or districts through instruments that are changed slightly from year to year. In contrast, at the institutional level the data base usually contains records for specific students, faculty, and staff members. A statistical data base thus has characteristics that are not compatible with institutional data processing systems. Usually statistical use requires integration of several files, reformatting to achieve compatibility with query languages and general statistical packages, and recoding or transforming some variables. For these reasons, the statistical use of a data base from an operating administrative application or the conversion of a data base from one form to another may be relatively expensive and therefore not adaptable to all institutional types.

The four data bases found most frequently at the institutional level and developed in part as an intermediate step when using the NCHEMS Costing and Data Management System are student, faculty and staff, budget and accounting, and facilities. The budget itself has rapidly become a major data base. Some institutions are now providing monthly budgets based on historical spending patterns and organizing the budget by organization, function, and object of expenditure.

The educational administrator should be aware that software tools for developing, documenting, and using statistical data bases now exist. These are neither complex nor expensive. The availability of these tools may assist the educational administrator in exploiting institutional data files for planning and management use.

Implementation Progress to Date

Planning and management systems offer several methods for improving the decision-making process in education, and many educational administrators are continuing to attend training sessions to acquire further insights into available systems. A number of schools, colleges, and universities have actually implemented these systems, though with varying degrees of success. While there are almost no published reviews of these implementations, some general observations can be made:

1. Planning and management systems usually depend upon data generated by administrative data systems or clerical processes. Typically, for institutions with enrollments over 1000 FTE students, the collection of data is usually too great a task unless there are compatible automated administrative systems.
2. Implementation success is inversely related to size. This means that large and costly systems are more likely to fail, either through declining user support, lack of resource, or natural obsolescence.
3. The most frequent motivating force is external requirements, usually from the state level. Conversely, there is little motivation for internal staffs to use accumulated data for management or planning.
4. A committed technical staff member may achieve a successful implementation; a committed executive usually achieves a successful implementation.
5. Frustration and fatigue, usually over technical problems of implementation, is the most frequent terminator of a systems implementation project.

It is important to recognize that there are several levels of implementation.[7] The developers usually define implementation as meaning that the computer programs have been installed and run on test data. The institutional data processors and institutional researchers usually mean that the computer programs have been installed, operate on test data, and some effort has been made to collect data. However, for the user, *implementation should mean that the original data has been collected, the computer programs installed, staff members have been trained in the use of the system and interpretation of the results, and useful results for decision making have been obtained.*

Implementation does not need to be elaborate or expensive. To provide some guidance to the costs of implementation, some estimated "person weeks" have been given for each major system in Table 3-1. These estimates are reasonable for a four-year institution with 2000 to 6000 students and some automated administrative systems. Both research universities and community colleges are more complex and usually require additional implementation effort. Institutions with operating administrative data systems will usually require less effort than those with manual systems or with administrative systems under development. In some cases, state implementation costs more than institutional implementation because of the larger number of institutions. On the other hand, it is sometimes more expensive at the institution since more detail may be required. Some models, like the tuition-access model, require external data that

Table 3-1
Estimated Typical Implementation Costs for Planning and Management Systems

Type of System	Level	Range of Estimated Cost (in person-weeks)	
		External	Internal
HEGIS Data Base	State	2.5-8.0	2.0-4.0
Cost and Data Management System	Institution	1.2-8.0	2.0-4.0
Outcomes	Institution	0.6-1.2	2.0-10.0
Facilities Utilization	State	8.0-16.0	8.0-24.0
	Institution	1.0-2.0	2.0-4.0
Faculty Utilization	State	8.0-12.0	8.0-24.0
	Institution	1.0-2.0	2.0-4.0
General Planning System	Institution	1.0-3.0	1.0-3.0
Student Flow Model	Institution	2.0-4.0	2.0-4.0
	State	6.0-12.0	4.0-50.0
RRPM	Institution	1.0-3.0	1.0-12.0
SPACE Model	Institution	3.2-6.4	1.5-8.0
Tuition Access	State	1.5-2.5	1.0-4.0
	Institution	1.0-3.0	1.0-8.0

may be unavailable. Outcomes data requires a survey; thus the cost of mail and telephone calls is directly proportional to the number of students and could be prohibitive for some institutions.

As mentioned, the executive who successfully implements such a system is usually one with a dedicated technical advisor, an efficient and effective data processing capability, and external requirements. The most frequent tactical error in implementation is to permit staff to encounter frustration or delay due to technical problems.

But the educational administrator may gain many of the benefits without actual implementation. Levels of participation include:

1. Study of the system to determine the underlying concepts and typical results.
2. Study of the results of an implementation at a similar institution with emphasis on the results confirmed as true and the results that disproved or questioned the validity of traditional interpretations.
3. Implementation in the institution as a one-time project.
4. Implementation in the institution as a continuing information requirement.

Often the first two are as rewarding and as useful as the last two, depending upon the institution and its needs. Clearly, continuing progress toward implementation will be most stimulated by external agencies and trustees or by administrators at large institutions who wish improved data for internal use.

The implementor has three sources of technical advice and assistance. Usually limited support is available from the developers. Individuals from institutions that have implemented the system may be available as consultants. Also, there are now specialists in implementation whose only function is assisting institutions. The need for outside assistance depends upon the capabilities of the institutional staff, the urgency for the implementation, the complexity of the system, and the availability of resources.

Summary

Very little is found in educational organizations that cannot be associated in some way with a systems approach. The use of this approach can assist in achieving a better understanding of the complexity of the structure of educational organizations, thus allowing us to deal with a relatively small number of fundamental variables. Hence, through the systems approach the structure and the problems of that structure can be studied with the hope of learning more about how the educational organization's social and economic characteristics combine to produce an educational output.

The educational administrator must have an in-depth understanding of the systems approach to determine the role it can play in providing insights into the planning and management of an educational organization. The administrator should be aware that these systems, properly used, may significantly improve his performance as a decision maker and thus improve the institution and its programs. However, the educational administrator should also be aware that the systems approach is only one perspective to the problems of an institution. It offers the possibility of increased understanding of the institutional processes, the capability of responding more quickly to information requirements, accountability, and a boundary for compromise on funding and instructional methodology issues.

Actual implementation may not be necessary; the educational administrator may gain considerable insight by studying the planning and management systems and their implementation at similar institutions. Implementation has many pitfalls, but resources are available to assist the administrator, and the benefits derived could far exceed the aggravations and frustrations experienced during the implementation period. At the very least, educational administrators owe it to themselves and their clients to investigate the possibility of using a planning and management systems approach in adjusting their campuses to times of financial exigency.

References

1. Colby H. Springer. *MICRO-U 70.1: Training Model of an Instructional Institution, Users Manual*, Technical Report 10. Boulder, Colorado: Western Interstate Commission for Higher Education, March 1970. See also Colby H. Springer. *A Pilot Implementation of the Cost Estimation Model at San Fernando Valley State College.* Los Angeles, California: Systems Research, Inc., February 1972.

2. Michael J. Haight and Ronald Martin. *NCHEMS Costing and Data Management System Documentation.* Boulder, Colorado: National Center for Higher Education Management Systems, January 1975.

3. David G. Clark, Robert Huff, Michael J. Haight, and William J. Collard. *Introduction to the Resource Requirements Prediction Model 1.6.* Boulder, Colorado: National Center for Higher Education Management Systems, 1973.

4. Robert Huff, et al. *Implementation of NCHEMS Planning and Management Tools at California State University-Fullerton.* Boulder, Colorado: National Center for Higher Education Management Systems, August 1972.

5. Daryle E. Carlson, James Farmer, and George B. Weathersby. *A Framework for Analyzing Postsecondary Education Financing Policies.* The National Commission on Financing of Postsecondary Education, May 1974.

6. See James Farmer. *An Approach to Planning and Management Systems*

Implementation. California State Colleges, January 1971. Also James Farmer and Talman Trask. *Outcome Measures for Community and Junior Colleges.* Los Angeles, California: Systems Research, Inc., November 1974.

7. For a project guide for costing, see Gary S. Gamso and Allan L. Service. *Introduction to Information Exchange Procedures: A Guide for the Project Manager.* Boulder, Colorado: National Center for Higher Education Management System, March 1976.

Introduction to Chapter 4

Faculty unions are here to stay, at least as long as problems of financial exigency continue to confront higher education. Most of the literature on faculty unions to date concerns the growth of faculty union movement and how to cope with a union organizational campaign. Little has been written about the strategies administrators should follow when confronted with demands by a faculty union for increased power over institutional decision making. Such demands are likely to arise once a union has negotiated several contracts or once it appears the employer simply has no access to more funds to meet union economic demands.

In this chapter Frank R. Kemerer suggests that administrators greet union demands for governance influence with a good deal of concern and care. How reflective of faculty concerns is the union? To what degree do faculty members wish to continue their professional involvement in academic decision making, as contrasted with their concerns as employees? What role should the union itself play in governance matters? A major part of the chapter is devoted to discussing practical strategies administrators should follow without jeopardizing the role of traditional deliberative bodies and the ability of the administration to respond to the challenges of financial exigency.

4 Responding to Union Demands for Governance Power

Frank R. Kemerer

Curricular specialization and the resulting proliferation of disciplinary departments, particularly since 1950, have made a campus deliberative forum increasingly necessary to provide a setting where members of the academy, both administrative and teaching, can come together to deliberate over institutional academic policy. A senate or similar body as a manifestation of shared governance becomes particularly important when financial exigency demands adjustments of institutional mission and programs. Since administrators may not know what academic programs ought to be excised or strengthened, the senate or a committee drawn from its membership rationalizes academic decision making by providing recommendations from those most involved in the work of the academy. Equally important, such widespread study and deliberation over program and personnel adjustments can provide administrators with the campus political support necessary to carry out painful decisions.

Into this complex governance arena has come the faulty union. What role is it to play? Initially, most unions confine their activities to purely economic matters. But with the passing of time, the interests of a faculty union tend to expand into the decision-making territory of other campus bodies. Some believe union involvement will prove beneficial for institutional governance.[1] But others are uneasy about growing union involvement and question the degree to which administrators and union leaders *can* cooperate, particularly when retrenchment decisions threaten job security.

The underlying assumption of this chapter is that with most of the institutional resources under their control, administrators have a unique opportunity to influence the role of the faculty union in campus governance. Because the educational institution is so dependent on the involvement of professionals to accomplish its mission, academic unions can be effective in improving the quality of academic decision making to the extent that they promote the professional involvement of their members. But unions have a life of their own. Despite rhetoric to the contrary, they do not have the same commitment to achieving institutional goals as do administrators. Nor do they have the same legal responsibility. For administrators to be effective in influencing the role of the union in campus governance, they must first understand the nature of faculty unions and their quest for governance power through the collective bargaining process. This is the purpose of the first part of the chapter. The scene then shifts to examine some of the specific ways in which administrators can shape the role of the faculty union in campus governance.

51

Unions and Their Quest for Governance Power

Unions are employee interest groups. Only those within the bargaining unit who pay dues can participate in union affairs. Internal decision making is conducted democratically—one person, one vote. The leadership is elected from the membership. This pattern is considerably different from traditional deliberative bodies in professional organizations where training and experience usually entitle some members to a disproportionate share of power. Thus, where unions and traditional deliberative bodies coexist, they are in a state of dynamic tension because they are dissimilar in nature and because their membership and leadership frequently do not overlap. Table 4-1 compares the major characteristics of unions to those of campus senates.

As an employee interest group, the union itself cannot be a body where administrators, faculty, and nonteaching professionals can deliberate over matters central to the educational profession. High-status academicians such as top administrators and department chairpersons are often excluded. A bargaining unit may be limited to a particular group of faculty, excluding others such as nonteaching professionals, part-time faculty, and professional school faculty. Students are excluded. Many faculty in the bargaining unit may not wish to pay dues (in the absence of a union security device such as an agency shop), and thus they are excluded from shaping union policy, though they receive the benefits of collective bargaining. In some cases, less than 30 percent of the bargaining unit is enrolled in the union. Claims that a union speaks for the entire faculty should thus be greeted with some degree of skepticism. Indeed, the senate may also not speak for a majority of the faculty on many issues, particularly those related to employment conditions.

Union Goals

Unions in higher education may seek governance power, as well as traditional economic benefits. In a 1974 Stanford study, the desire for more influence in campus governance was rated a significant factor in bringing about unionization at the 300 campuses studied.[2] As studies of contract content illustrate, unions in higher education are slowly succeeding in expanding their jurisdiction into governance areas.[3,4]

A leading cause for the expansion of union concern, of course, relates to the need on many campuses for rapid adjustment in programs and personnel to the demands of financial exigency. Naturally, a union must by its nature respond to the demands of its members for a greater say in decisions affecting their employment.

The nature of the union and the selection of the leadership are also related to union policy. Union leaders are elected from the membership and obviously

Table 4-1
Faculty Unions and Senates Contrasted

Characteristic	Union	Senate
Basic theoretical foundation	One employee group selected as exclusive agent for bargaining with the employer over wages, hours, and other terms of employment.	Deliberative forum for members of the academic profession to formulate and recommend academic policy for the educational institution.
External legal framework	Necessary to structure the bargaining process and demand the employer's attention.	Not necessary.
Membership	All employees within the bargaining unit are eligible to become members; only those who pay dues can be voting members, though in some instances, nonunion employees may be allowed to vote on a final negotiated contract.	Direct or proportional participation, the latter usually based on relative size of academic department. Often the college president serves as the chairman since he or she is the educational leader of the institution. High status members, e.g., tenured professors, are apt to be represented more than their relative numbers would indicate. In recent years students and representatives from other groups are often included in senates, making them more reflective of the campus as an academic community.
Internal governance	Union leaders, union policy, and the adoption of a contract are usually determined by democratic vote of the dues-paying membership. Much of union strategy is developed in representative study groups. Often, a union professional and staff will be employed to coordinate day-to-day affairs.	Most of the work is done in committees, with Roberts Rules of Order governing the work of these bodies and the procedure of the senate as a whole.
Most useful image	Formal interest group.	Upper chamber of a legislature.

realize some satisfaction and status from their role. They and the union seek to retain high visibility as a "can-do" group in the eyes of the membership. This is particularly critical during a long-term contract when the rhetoric and headlines of past bargaining talks fade.

If union leaders and the union itself disappear from view, many dues-paying members will begin wondering why they should continue to pay anywhere from

$100 to $300 annually in membership fees. They may decide more aggressive leaders should be chosen.

Other major variables affecting the union quest for governance power include the following:

1. *Past governance tradition.* Faculties who have enjoyed substantial governance influence will be more inclined to restrict their union to economic matters or use it to shore up traditional governance bodies.

2. *The level of faculty professionalism.* If faculty members view themselves as highly professional, they will be less inclined to allow the union to encroach on departmental and senate prerogatives. As with strong governance tradition, a high degree of faculty professionalism may cause the membership to use the union to strengthen existing deliberative bodies. This has occurred at several institutions, including Southeastern Massachusetts University, Rutgers University, and Temple University.

3. *The level of union membership.* Contrary to the fears of many administrators, there is evidence that high union membership fosters better, more stable management-labor relations. Low membership can force the administration to retain or develop a strong academic senate to co-opt the union and obtain needed input from academicians at the same time. However, low membership also may promote senate-union rivalry. There is a growing belief among those who study academic bargaining that the best of all worlds for deliberative bodies is a high level of faculty professionalism coupled with high union membership.

4. *Senate-union leadership qualities.* The leaders and political power of the two agencies will determine their degree of cooperation. At Southeastern Massachusetts University, the leaders of both senate and union have been instrumental in determining the respective responsibilities of their organizations and promoting mutual accommodation.

5. *Administrative-faculty value consensus.* A consensus of views among administrators and faculty members about the outcomes of the highly political bargaining process will help assimilate the union into the governance structure. Unfortunately, harsh environmental pressures, value diversity among differing categories of those labeled "faculty," and growing centralization of decision making make consensus less likely on most campuses.

6. *Single-campus-multicampus systems.* It is easier to negotiate an accommodation between union and senate at the single campus institution. In fact, those campuses where "collegiality by contract" appears to be a reality are usually single campuses. The multicampus system makes negotiations on local governance problems difficult, if not impossible.

7. *The approach of campus administrators.* This will be the major concern of the last part of this chapter.

Union Tactics

The tactics unions use will, of course, differ. At the bargaining table, most unions will demand negotiation over all *mandatory* topics of bargaining, that is, issues that *must* be negotiated if one side wishes to discuss them. At the same time, they will seek to *expand* the list of mandatory items, particularly if they affect job security in hard times. For example, at the City University of New York (CUNY), the Professional Staff Congress tried to get student evaluation of faculty classified as a mandatory item for negotiation in 1974. At Rutgers, the AAUP in 1975 sought to have a whole list of items classified as mandatory bargaining topics, including the university's budget, class size, changes in physical facilities, tenure quotas, studies of faculty productivity, and inclusion of faculty members on search committees for administrators. For three years beginning in 1973, the faculty association at Central Michigan University fought a legal battle to get evaluation of faculty members classified as a mandatory bargaining issue and accused the administration of unfair labor practice in dealing only with the institutional senate. In all these instances, the unions failed to convince the state labor boards. Thus, these issues remain *permissive* issues, that is, both sides must agree to bargain over them. In effect, they are matters of management prerogative, though by tradition they are often delegated to the academic senate.

Most unions will also seek to have administrators bargain over permissive topics. Thus, the union at SUNY in 1976 sought to include this clause on campus bylaws in the new contract:

Each academic or professional department, subdivision, division, school, and college shall deliberate and formulate its own policies, procedures, and decisions on curricular matters, course offerings, personnel matters, appraisal of goals and objectives, and budgetary matters in accordance with basic democratic procedures, all of which shall be implemented in a consistent and non-discriminatory manner.

By this phrase, campus bylaws would shift from being a management prerogative under Trustee *Policies* to being the prerogative of the faculty. While reasonable enough at first glance, the implications are enormous. First, giving departments the power to develop bylaws coupled with the union insistence on "democratic procedures" would effectively terminate the role of the administration in academic governance, particularly where personnel decisions are involved. High-level administrators have a right, even an obligation, to participate in these matters. To the extent that they can change the procedures used to reach academic decisions, including personnel appointments, through the *approval power* of bylaws, they are fulfilling a professional responsibility. Second, democratizing campus bylaws would curtail the influence of high-status, high-rank faculty. Presumably, in education, as in other professions, status and rank entitle one to a greater share of decision-making power.

There are numerous other ways a union can extend its influence through the negotiation of new contracts. The Cook County Teachers Union succeeded in incorporating a strait-jacket, past-practice clause in the first contract with the City Colleges of Chicago. At Rutgers University and in the Pennsylvania State College System, the union has sought to establish "study committees" to explore governance-related issues outside of the negotiation procedure. In the Minnesota State University System, the NEA union succeeded in abolishing senates in 1976, replacing them with a union committee structure on both the campus and system level. On some campuses, unions have not sought to terminate traditional governance structures but to dominate them instead.

Once a contract is signed, the union will likely shift to the grievance system, long regarded as another channel through which unions can enlarge their influence. Since the union has an exclusive right to represent the employees in a bargaining unit, does the administration commit an unfair labor practice in dealing with traditional governance structures? Some unions have asserted the affirmative, though recent PERB decisions have not taken this position. Another area where unions seek to expand their influence is challenges to personnel decisions. Even when the contract is silent on the criteria to be used in the evaluation of faculty members, unions will challenge adverse decisions. At the State University of New York (SUNY), for example, the substantive criteria for continuing appointments have been outlined in the *Policies of the Board of Trustees*, not addressed in the union contract. Only the procedural steps have been grievable. Thus, the union has had limited access to departmental and divisional personnel decisions. Nevertheless, the union has repeatedly accused the administration of undermining peer evaluation and academic due process in denying tenure to faculty and in retrenchment of faculty. Judgments are said to be trivial, irrelevant, factually incorrect, and a clear indication of arbitrary decision making based on subjective standards and unannounced criteria. In the 1976 list of bargaining demands, the SUNY union avoided including substantive criteria in the section on personnel decision making but elsewhere demanded that "no employee shall be reduced in rank, suffer a loss of professional advantage or benefit, or loss of employment, or be reprimanded or disciplined without just cause." Since academic personnel decisions are hard to quantify, given the subjectivity of the teaching-learning-counseling process, acceptance of this provision would give the union control of substantive personnel decision making without incorporating substantive criteria into the contract!

So far, unions have been successful in expanding contractual coverage, but not because they have consistently won in the courts or before public employment relations boards (PERBS). As we have seen, contracts expand for many reasons, some of which can be strongly influenced by administrative action.

Administrative Response Strategies

The first concern is whether to aggressively oppose union governance demands or seek to accommodate them. On some matters, such as the selection and remuneration of administrators, unions should not be allowed to negotiate under any circumstances. Indeed, given their vested interest as employees at the bargaining table, one questions whether a unionized faculty should participate in administrative searches at all. But aside from topics clearly identified as matters of essential administrative prerogative, how should administrators react to union demands for governance influence?

Opposing Union Demands for Governance Power

Where union membership is low and faculty professionalism high, active support for deliberative bodies will probably be quite evident among most of the faculty. Union membership is likely to be confined to a particular faculty group. Obviously, unions in this situation are struggling for visibility and support; they may resent administrative deference toward academic departments and the campus senate. Faced with continuous union demands for greater involvement in governance, administrators on these campuses are best off opposing such demands both at the bargaining table and during periodic consultation sessions under the contract until they are sure union demands truly reflect the wishes of the majority of the faculty. How many faculty members actually belong to the union? Of those that do, is union policy geared to their interests or to the concerns of the faculty as a whole? How is the union policy developed? One way to find answers to these questions is to take advantage of much of the research now being conducted by faculty and student groups on collective bargaining practices at their own campus. In any event, until it is clear that a majority of the faculty wish the union to negotiate over governance issues, bargaining should be restricted to economic issues insofar as possible under the law. Academic matters, including programmatic issues related to retrenchment, should be clearly identified as the prerogative of departments, campus senates, ad hoc committees, and the administration. On campuses where there is a high level of consensus, the jurisdiction of these bodies might be outlined in the union contract and will thus effectively delineate the role of both the union and the senate. Other strategies include adopting an aggressive management posture by initiating demands, asking union representatives to explain the rationale behind their proposals, insisting that every concession made to the union has a price (quid pro quo), developing the means to calculate the long-range implications of agreements, and aggressively advancing the administrative position before labor boards, arbitrators, and courts.

While administrators should remain neutral toward the internal politics of unions to avoid an unfair labor practice charge and to forestall alienating much of the faculty, they can be sensitive to the direction of political power on campus and take the lead to cool union-senate conflict through informal discussions. At the same time, they should promote the involvement of deliberative forums in the complexities of governance. In some cases, of course, the faculty union will endorse administrative involvement with faculty forums, partly because the lack of involvement may have been a prime factor in bringing about the union and partly because union leaders realize the union is not capable of meeting every faculty need. Mortimer and Gershenfeld report from their study of forty Pennsylvania campuses that many contracts provide for the establishment of deliberative forums where administrators and faculty members can meet to discuss academic problems.[5] This pattern is more likely to occur, however, at institutions where the union membership significantly overlaps that of the senate or where the union overtly supports the senate.

Accommodating Union Demands for Governance Power

Where union membership is high, administrative strategies in dealing with the union are more limited, regardless of the level of faculty professionalism. To oppose the union is to jeopardize administrative credibility with the faculty. Administrators in this situation must seek to establish some degree of accommodation with the union. Where faculty professionalism and union membership are both high, administrators may have a good chance of winning union support simply by seriously involving the faculty senate in vital institutional decision making. Southeastern Massachusetts and St. John's University are testimony to the success of this approach. But where the level of faculty professionalism is low, unions, whether strong or weak, may refuse to back administrative efforts to develop or to strengthen deliberative bodies. To "stonewall" the union under these circumstances is to invite waves of conflict that could weaken or even eliminate administrative influence. However, it might be possible to win union support for a committee system established jointly by the union and the administration to operate outside of the bargaining arena. At the Pennsylvania State College System, negotiators set up two such committees in 1974, one to study promotion procedures and the other tenure. According to the contract, both committees would consist of two members named by the union, two by the Board of College Presidents, and two by the Secretary of Education (the employer). Unions will struggle mightily to secure great influence, if not controlling influence in these committees. This is particularly true where retrenchment issues are involved.[6] If union leaders oppose deliberative bodies and joint committees because they are advisory and seek instead a governance role for themselves, administrators should consider refusing such demands, even if it means embracing a management prerogative stance. Yielding to union demands could subject administrative decisions to union veto. A two-year college agreement in Washington State provides that the long-range planning and budget development policies of the college are negotiable and that disagreements are subject to binding arbitration. One wonders what the union will do in the next round of negotiations! Administrators can always establish ad hoc study groups outside the contractual relationship for input and support on difficult institutional problems. Many unions are taking the position that retrenchment-related decisions are decisions for management anyway. While such a position is clearly contrary to the professional image college professors nurture, it does give management the initiative to make such decisions and confines the union to a reactive role through the grievance system or the courts, as is characteristic of unions in nonprofessional organizational settings. Of course, where faculty members cooperate with management in retrenchment decision making, they have not necessarily given up their right to grieve subsequent actions.

To summarize, where union membership is low and faculty professionalism high, administrators should show strong support for deliberative bodies and be suspicious of union demands for greater governance influence. Conversely, where union membership is high, administrators must establish some accommodation with union demands regardless of the level of faculty professionalism if administrative credibility is to be maintained.

Influencing System-Level Administrators

In systems of education, contract bargainers are usually system-level administrators. Occasionally, bargaining is the responsibility of the state department of education as at the Pennsylvania State College System or a branch of the governor's office as at SUNY. In these instances, it is crucial for campus-level administrators to help shape the outcomes of bargaining talks, for it is they who will be held directly accountable for quality, efficiency, and uninterrupted service at the campus level. In many systems, central authorities do not ask for input from campus-level administrators, and campus presidents are lax in demanding that they be consulted before decisions are made. In the fourteen-campus Pennsylvania State College System, for example, some college presidents have bitterly assailed the Department of Education officials in Harrisburg for ignoring campus presidents in favor of accommodating more powerful union interests. As one president complained recently, "We have become little more than third-rate functionaries while Harrisburg has gotten in bed with the union." Campus administrators are also often lax in securing ironclad support from central officials to sustain campus leaders through the high levels of conflict generated by implementing unpopular contractual and noncontractual policies and procedures. A prime example of what can happen when faculty-administrative conflict breaks into the open is well illustrated by the exit of President Gail Parker from Bennington in 1976 after an unsuccessful attempt to manage financial exigency at her institution.[7]

Off-campus influence, of course, should not stop with system-level administrators. Campus officials also need to influence the decisions reached by labor boards, state education "superboards," and even the state legislature. Callan and

Jonsen in Chapter 9 discuss the growing importance of state coordinating agencies, and Angell in Chapter 7 offers some illuminating advice on developing an effective legislative communications program.

Rationalizing Campus Administration

The most adept posture at the bargaining table will fail in the long run if ineffective internal operating procedures provoke faculty to turn increasingly to their union for help. Since administrators are at the hub of campus activities, they stand in the best position to remove the mystery of campus governance by promoting a clarification of governance roles. We have already noted that administrators are in a strategic position to affect the relationship between senate and union. One commentator has noted that after the rejection of bargaining at Michigan State University in the fall of 1972, senior professors and sympathetic administrators moved to strengthen the hold of the faculty-administrative oligarchy on academic governance. As a result, this commentator notes that the frustration of junior faculty members will only be rectified by "a stronger collective bargaining movement more cognizant of the noneconomic interests and the Florentine politics of research-oriented universities such as Michigan State."[8] At many campuses, such as Michigan's Albion College, a small Methodist Church-related institution, the administration has taken the opposite tack by promoting wider participation in deliberative bodies at the expense of faculty oligarchies so as to co-opt further pressures for unionization. One suspects that the latter approach will provide a greater defense against renewed efforts to unionize.

In addition to promoting wider participation in governance and clarifying the roles of various campus constituencies, administrators should see that their own administrative hierarchy is functioning effectively to resolve problems before they magnify. Are communication channels open and uncluttered from the supervisory level to the top level of management? Are noncontractual procedures and mechanisms adequate for channeling and resolving personnel problems? The development of effective parallel channels for the resolution of problems not covered by the contractual grievance system will dampen faculty sentiment for having the union negotiate in these areas. Are the administrators who deal directly with the faculty sensitive, capable, and respected? A recent study of nine diverse institutions with faculty unions indicates that the personalities and philosophies of both management and union officials have a lot to do with the degree to which unionism has been assimilated into the governance structure.[9] On several campuses included in the study, the main reason for continued high conflict over the role of the union is the unwillingness of key administrators to accept faculty collective bargaining as a permanent fixture on the campus, even though a large percentage of the faculty had voted for a union. Antiunion bias that is allowed to creep into conferences with faculty members or be aired in "confidential" high-level management sessions plays directly into the hands of prounion forces. In sum, the level of trust in the administration bears an inverse relationship with bargaining sentiment. High trust is encouraged by open communication *within* the administrative hierarchy and *between* the administration and the faculty. Of course, deeds speak louder than words. Trust will not develop until administrators promote it.

One way to assess management problems and develop more effective campus administration is to schedule periodic in-service educational programs for the "management team." Indiana University in Pennsylvania recently inaugurated an in-service training program for some thirty top managers, including the president, six vice-presidents, eight deans, and a number of associate deans and other campus officials. Not only do these intensive in-service sessions enable members of the management team to develop a common identity, they also provide administrators with important information from on-campus and off-campus sources which undoubtedly will make them more effective at carrying out their respective managerial duties. As one member of the Indiana seminar points out, "It also gives top leaders the chance to detect weak links in the management constituency."

Involving Students in Collective Bargaining

Unions are generally opposed to student participation, even though nearly half of a recent national sample of faculty members endorsed student participation in faculty hiring and promotion decisions.[10] Student participation in prebargaining and postbargaining briefing sessions may make union demands for governance influence more responsive to campus realities. This is not to suggest that student demands for an independent right to bargain with the administration should be granted or that administrators should be paternalistic toward students. Nor does this suggestion imply that failure to recognize students will amount to overlooking a natural ally. But giving students a limited role in collective bargaining with the faculty may defuse much of the antagonism students often feel toward the administration, though admittedly at the risk of increasing faculty resentment. It may even cause students to look more critically on what many consider the natural alliance of students with the faculty.

If students are not accorded a role in the faculty bargaining process, they may well escalate their efforts to achieve a bargaining status of their own, a situation bound to complicate administration by increasing campus balkanization. Already several states including Montana, Oregon, and Maine have responded to powerful student lobbies by granting students a limited role in faculty negotiations. Some student groups are now seeking a statutory right to bargain on an independent basis regardless of their employment status.[11]

Conclusion

Unionization and the forces behind its growth clearly force administrators into the unfamiliar and sometimes uncomfortable role of "management." While administrators must be concerned about faculty support, many of today's decisions will not please all or even most faculty members. Once administrators realize that they cannot always please the faculty without bankrupting the institution or destroying their own credibility with other agencies, they will be more effective in shaping campus patterns of academic governance to the realities of unionization. In some instances, a majority of the faculty will expect the union to play a limited role in governance matters. To be unduly solicitous of union leaders under these circumstances will antagonize many faculty members and weaken existing governance structures unnecessarily. In other instances the old way will no longer work. To refuse to share past management prerogatives or to struggle to support deliberative bodies may be a fruitless effort, which only serves to antagonize most of the faculty and their union. Yet yielding to union demands may effectively hand campus administration over to union leaders. In short, while faculty support for administrative decision making must remain a strong concern, that concern needs to be more discriminating and pragmatic.

At the same time that the best bargaining strategy is being formed based on the level of faculty professionalism and extent of union membership, effort has to be devoted to strengthening administrative influence on off-campus bodies, particularly those that fund the institution, shape the bargaining framework, and adjudicate union-management disputes. On the campus, administrators need to streamline administrative procedures and practices to promote maximum confidence and trust among faculty and staff. Antiunion bias must be supressed. First-level administrators need to be among the most skilled in interpersonal relations and conflict management. Finally, administrators should investigate how the bargaining process might involve students, the ones often most affected by bargaining outcomes. While it is, of course, not possible to predict that campus governance will cease to be a troublesome issue if these suggestions are followed, it is possible to predict that adopting these strategies will likely make the task easier.

References

1. Donald E. Walker, David Feldman, and Greg Stone. "Collegiality and Collective Bargaining: An Alternative Perspective." *Educational Record*, Spring 1976.

2. Frank R. Kemerer and J. Victor Baldridge. *Unions on Campus: A National Study of The Consequences of Faculty Bargaining.* San Francisco: Jossey-Bass, 1975, chapter 3.

3. Harold I. Goodwin and Edwin R. Smith (eds.). *Encyclopedia of Collective Bargaining.* Morgantown, West Virginia: The West Virginia University Bookstore, 1975.

4. Robert H. Kellett. "Trends and Patterns of Change in Public Community College Collective Bargaining Contracts." Washington, D.C.: Academic Collective Bargaining Information Service, September 1975.

5. Walter J. Gershenfeld and Kenneth P. Mortimer. *Faculty Collective Bargaining in Pennsylvania (1970-1975).* Philadelphia: Center for Labor and Manpower Studies, Temple University, 1976

6. Harold I. Goodwin and John R. Pisapia (eds.). "Committees and Job Security." *Collective Bargaining Perspectives*, Vol. 1, No. 1, 1975. (Publication of the Department of Educational Administration at West Virginia University, Morgantown.)

7. Nora Ephron. "The Bennington Affair." *Esquire*, September 1976.

8. Henry Perlstadt. "Faculty Oligarchy and Union Democracy." Paper prepared for the 24th Annual Meeting of the Society for the Study of Social Problems, August 23, 1975.

9. Ronald P. Satryb. "The Art of Settling Grievances: A Study in Conflict Resolution." Washington, D.C.: Academic Collective Bargaining Information Service, August 1976.

10. E.C. Ladd and S.M. Lipset. "Students in Campus Decision-Making: What Do Faculty Members Think?" *The Chronicle of Higher Education*, March 22, 1976.

11. See Chip Berlet (ed.). *Student Unionization: Perspectives on Establishing A Union Of Students.* Washington, D.C.: National Student Association, 1975.

Introduction to Chapter 5

The ultimate result of serious financial exigency will be programmatic and personnel retrenchment. These actions are the most difficult to face and initiate. The excisement of programs steeped in tradition and of personnel with families and friends will provide administrators with a most difficult task. Chapter 5 provides guidelines for undertaking appropriate institutional actions to minimize retrenchment trauma.

Ronald P. Satryb discusses the legal and procedural basis for retrenchment action with particular attention to AAUP guidelines and collective bargaining restrictions. The roles of various institutional constituencies are explored. A detailed, step-by-step plan of action is presented for accomplishing the retrenchment process efficiently and effectively with a minimum of institutional and individual disruption. Even allowing for institutional differences, readers will find this chapter enlightening in exploring this most difficult of financial exigency problems.

5

Planning for Personnel and Programmatic Retrenchment

Ronald P. Satryb

Two of the most frightening terms in the academy today are "financial exigency" and "retrenchment." There is no question that dwindling support—both financial and political—poses a very real crisis for both private and public higher education. The era of the Jerry Browns and Hugh Careys has arrived with apparent support from the voters. Public higher education is a prime target for budget cuts and is being pushed further down the priorities list in many states. Private education is also caught in a trap of declining enrollments and increasing costs. More and more institutions are being forced to retrench both personnel and programs.

The fiscal crisis at particular institutions may be immediate or may have developed over a long period. There will often be conflict between the faculty and administration concerning the existence and extent of the crisis. In any event, a financial crisis must be met with fairness and with a primary concern for institutional objectives.

The following discussion will outline a plan of action that highlights some of the pitfalls administrators will have to face. However, blanket application of these steps would ignore the individual characteristics of institutions throughout higher education. Clearly, the character of the institution should determine to what extent the guidelines may be applied in any particular instance.

Participants in Retrenchment Planning

Can willing participants in the retrenchment game be found on the local campus beyond a group called "management"? The myth of collegiality would seem to dictate an answer—but one that must be seriously examined in view of the new realities in higher education. Collegiality presents visions of shared governance, democratic decision making and consensus planning for the good of the whole. To what extent this type of system ever actually existed on any campus is open to debate. In any case, the growth of unionism in higher education must be considered in the world of retrenchment and financial exigency. Many think of unionism in higher education as the dramatic but slow expansion of faculty unions. This is an important factor, but the spread of unionism to other employee groups on campus such as professionals, trades employees, and service employees must be considered equally important. Every gain in monetary and fringe benefits by each campus employee group adds to the cost of education.

With personnel costs rapidly approaching 85 percent of many university budgets, there can be little doubt where the high cost of education rests. Every commitment on workload, programs, or procedures has a fiscal impact. Unions add one more element to the crisis of retrenchment which is not found at nonunionized campuses.

In better times, whatever degree of traditional collegiality was present on any campus involved such things as faculty promotions, hiring, granting of tenure, approval of courses, and expansion of programs. The dullest and least sought-after assignments were often the budget and long-range planning committees. Everything was short range because the "horn of plenty" was ever present and faculty mobility precluded much interest in institutional planning beyond that of one's own discipline. What appeared to be unlimited prospects for expansion allowed everyone to wear "white hats" without concern for attendant responsibilities. The educational professions became self-perpetuating with the rapid growth of state systems and community colleges. Decentralized governance systems were expanded even to the old state teachers colleges that had gone "liberal arts." Fledgling faculty unions were expected to be co-opted into the system. Administrators were not forced to take aggressive leadership roles since their function was often a simple matter of requesting budgetary increases to implement the democratically conceived expansionary goals of the faculty. This overstatement is presented to underline the point that those conditions no longer exist today in most of the large public university systems. The private sector has had to face the economic realities sooner and on a more individual basis.

Given current realities, the decision-making process has removed the "white hats" from all of the participants. While each institution will have its own experiences with the faculty and staff in a period of retrenchment, it is already clear that active participation by faculty in the establishment of retrenchment units may come reluctantly, if at all. Some unions have left the retrenchment decisions to management so that they could be free to fight those decisions before arbitrators and the courts. Retrenchment, unionism, accountability, and program budgeting have all done their part to force the academic administrator into the role of "manager." The expansionist administrators of the past in both the private and public sectors have either had to adapt to this new role or move to new assignments.

The traditional decentralized governance pattern and the new more centralized approach have been fused together in a confusing and complicated way. Traditional collegial processes now coexist uneasily with highly technical programmatic planning systems. The latter deal with costs per student, full-time equivalent (FTE), square footage, and contact hours. There are national networks of hardware, software, and technical consultants. Local campuses have computer specialists, business managers, and institutional researchers. The collegial process uses some data, but relies more on reasoned debate and scholarly opinion to arrive at conclusions to benefit the institution and its constituencies. Now many faculty are excluded from the entire budgetary and planning process by the esoteric nature of the new systems, as well as by provincial faculty concern with their academic discipline. It is doubtful that collegial processes will ever again be truly dominant on many campuses, given the new complications of adjusting to an unsteady state.

Where unionism has appeared, a personal conflict for the faculty over whether they are professionals or employees has rapidly followed. Quite often they must switch back and forth between the two roles according to the circumstances. However, in a period of retrenchment they will, in some cases, tend to view themselves as employees to avoid participation in any program that will eventually eliminate them or their peers.[1] Whatever participation there is can rapidly deteriorate into a "get them, save us" syndrome. In other words, make the cuts in that other department, in the clerical staff, in administrative ranks, among the counselors, and so on. A union may choose to participate only through the negotiation of the impact of retrenchment, thereafter preferring to grieve management decisions. At other institutions, the faculty or its union may take an active part in the planning process as, for example, at Oakland University. This participation is to be preferred if the time exists for extended deliberation to benefit the total organization. But in the end, those who get paid to make the hard decisions will ultimately have to make those decisions, with or without consultation.

Preimplementation Stage

In a period of retrenchment, the roles of both unions and the courts[2] will be expanded. The 1976 massive retrenchments in SUNY and CUNY have resulted in a multitude of court suits brought both by unions and individuals. This development will help increase the power of managers. The unions will be moving strongly for job security provisions and as a group or as individuals will increasingly turn to the courts to protect their gains.[3] Since managers will be required to answer for their actions in the courts or through legal collective bargaining agreements, they will be less willing to share their responsibilities and decision-making powers. However, local unit managers may lose some of their powers in multicampus systems where a central administration may be reluctant to delegate responsibilities. This can be true in both the public and private sectors. In the public sector, legislators can have a profound effect on the requirements that managers may have to follow.

Retrenchment Provisions

Any manager faced with a fiscal crisis or a realignment of programs will need the tools to operate with either formally or informally. On the nonunionized campus this could mean nothing more than the confidence and backing of the board of trustees. At the unionized campus, the managers are bound by the provisions of any retrenchment or layoff procedures in the contract. Managers in both types of institutions should have access to competent legal advice since their personnel decisions stand an excellent chance of ultimate resolution in the courts.[4] It can be readily anticipated that individuals losing their positions in a poor labor market will resort to every available mechanism to defend themselves and retain their positions.

The retrenchment or layoff procedure should provide employees protection from arbitrary and capricious acts and still give the employer maximum flexibility. The latter concept is in direct opposition to the job security goals of any responsible union. Therefore, the contractualized retrenchment provision is likely to be one of the most controversial and difficult to negotiate. Nonunionized campuses will depend on local governance mechanisms, new trustees policies, or AAUP statements. The problems that can occur with the retrenchment provision can best be seen by contrasting the 1976 AAUP recommended Institutional Regulations on Academic Freedom and Tenure[5] with a contractualized retrenchment article.

The 1976 statement combines elements of the "1940 Statement of Principles on Academic Freedom and Tenure" and of the "1958 Statement on Procedural Standards in Faculty Dismissal Proceedings."

Financial Exigency. (c) (1) Termination of an appointment with continuous tenure, or of a probationary or special appointment before the end of the specified term, may occur under extraordinary circumstances because of a demonstrably bona fide financial exigency, i.e., an imminent financial crisis which threatens the survival of the institution as a whole and which cannot be alleviated by less drastic means. . . .

As a first step, there should be a faculty body which participates in the decision that a condition of financial exigency exists or is imminent, and that all feasible alternatives to termination of appointments have been pursued. . . .

Judgments determining where within the overall academic program termination of appointments may occur involve considerations of educational policy, including affirmative action, as well as of faculty status, and should therefore be the primary responsibility of the faculty or of an appropriate faculty body. . . .

The responsibility for identifying individuals whose appointments are to be terminated should be committed to a person or group designated or approved by the faculty. . . .

(2) If the administration issues notice to a particular faculty member of an intention to terminate the appointment because of financial exigency, the faculty member will have the right to a full hearing before a faculty committee. . . .

The issues in this hearing may include: (i) The existence and extent of a condition of financial exigency. The burden will rest on the administration to prove the existence and extent of the condition. The findings of a faculty committee in a previous proceeding involving the same issue may be introduced. (ii) The validity of the educational judgments and the criteria for identification for termination; but the recommendations of a faculty body on these matters will be considered presumptively valid. (iii) Whether the criteria are being properly applied in the individual case. . . .

(6) In all cases of termination of appointment because of financial exigency, the place of the faculty member concerned will not be filled by a replacement within a period of three years unless the released faculty member has been offered reinstatement and a reasonable time in which to accept or decline it. . . .

If the appointment is terminated, the faculty member will receive salary or notice in accordance with the following schedule: at least three months, if the final decision is reached by March 1 (or three months prior to the expiration) of the first year of probationary service; at least six months, if the decision is reached by December 15 of the second year (or after nine months but prior to eighteen months) of probationary service; at least one year, if the decision is reached after eighteen months of probationary service if the faculty member has tenure. . . .[6]

One of the sections of the AAUP statement that may be of major concern to managers involves required notifications. The three-month and six-month notice for certain employees is not unreasonable. However, the twelve-month notice for other employees may result in an extension of the financial crisis to a larger number of retrenchees. A long notice period may extend into subsequent budget years and, therefore, prolong the problem. Also, without an immediate reduction in costs, more individuals may have to be retrenched to achieve the required savings. Good personnel practice would dictate maximum notice to employees who have rendered long and loyal service. On the other hand, good fiscal policy would require a balanced budget immediately. In the case of public institutions, this may even be required by law. These two contradicting policies must somehow be brought into balance. However, managers should avoid negotiations on the definition of "financial exigency" and a "due process" retrenchment clause in the interest of maintaining flexibility to meet a financial crisis. The right to a "full hearing" added to extensive notice will create extensive budgetary problems through the extension of the time necessary to resolve the crisis.

By way of contrast, Article 35 of the faculty and professional staff contract at the State University of New York (1974-76) has avoided some of these danger areas.[7] Pertinent parts of that article are stated as follows:

Retrenchment shall be defined . . . as a result of financial exigency, reallocation of resources, reorganization of degree or curriculum offerings or requirements, reorganization of academic or administrative structures, programs or functions or curtailment of one or more programs or functions University-wide or at such level of organization of the University as a campus, department, unit, program or such other level of organization of the University as the Chancellor or his designee deems appropriate. . . . The Chancellor or his designee . . . shall apply retrenchment among employees holding the same or similar positions subject to retrenchment at such level or organization in inverse order of appointment within each affected group of employees hereinafter referred to, as follows: (a) Part-time employees before full-time employees. (b) Full-time academic employees holding term appointments before those holding continuing appointments. (c) Full-time professional employees holding term appointments before those holding permanent appointment. . . . The State will notify the persons affected by retrenchment as soon as practicable recognizing that, where circumstances permit, it is desirable to provide the following notice of termination: (a) For those holding term appointment, at least four months. (b) For those holding a continuing or permanent appointment, at least one semester. . . . For a period of two years following retrenchment, an employee removed as a result of retrenchment who is not otherwise employed in the University shall be offered re-employment in the same or similar position at the campus at which he was employed at the time of retrenchment should an opportunity for such re-employment arise. . . .

It is readily apparent that this article, unlike the AAUP statement, gives management a great deal of latitude to determine both when retrenchment is necessary and how it shall be applied. Yet as in the AAUP statement, the seniority of the employees is protected within specifically named categories. In general, while both the AAUP recommendation and the SUNY article have similarities, the AAUP recommendation may create problems for management through the extended notification requirements and the inclusion of extensive faculty participation and due process procedures. Much will depend, of course, on the characteristics of an institution, its administrative priorities, and its faculty.

The SUNY procedure allows either four-months' notice or one-semester's notice. However, it is important to note that this is not a requirement. The article stipulates that this notice is "desirable" if possible in the judgment of management. Thus, management is allowed the flexibility of keeping the retrenchment actions within any particular fiscal year. This also allows for the retention of more employees since the economic impact of any retrenchment action is more immediate. Good personnel practices are maintained by providing the maximum possible notice to the employee within any given circumstance. This approach would be preferable from the standpoint of any management team. However, where unions exist, it is well to remember that the retrenchment article will be achieved only through extensive negotiations and compromise.

Maintaining Communication

Retrenchment, like other actions that have a direct effect on the various parts of an institution, should be well thought out and thoroughly planned. This requires maximum input from all available internal and external campus constituencies. The input should be received through a consultation mechanism that is clear to everyone. One of the many problems involved in asking for advice is that the contributors expect you to take their suggestions! The president of a university cannot delegate his responsibilities in this area and must constantly reiterate that the final decision is his or hers to make.

Actions to be arrived at through consultation should have their beginning in the programmatic parameters of the institution. All decisions for eventual retrenchment of personnel and curtailment of programs should have a programmatic base. The curriculum of the institution which reflects its goals and character should be preserved in spite of severe financial excisement. Therefore, a review of institutional programs is a crucial preliminary step to a consideration of a reduction in force. Consultation through faculty, student, and administrative interaction is usually slow and sometimes agonizing. It is imperative that a timeline calendar for decision making be constructed and adhered to by all parties. It must be made clear to everyone involved in the consultation process that decisions will have to be made according to the calendar and that the demands of retrenchment do not lend themselves to lengthy delay.

Although various bodies may be assigned specific tasks in the consultation process, it is crucial that they not be allowed to operate in isolation. Each constituency should be expected to examine its own area and make appropriate recommendations or priorities. However, each constituency should also be required to examine one or two other areas and make recommendations on the priorities of that area. For example, the faculty may examine academic areas plus student affairs and business affairs. This exercise has a twofold purpose that may be beneficial beyond the crisis of the moment. The first and perhaps more obvious benefit of this procedure is educational. It is always helpful to have others evaluate one's contribution to the institution. This is especially applicable in nonacademic areas. Too often, everyone from campus cleaner to financial aids officer is taken for granted or unobserved completely. As a result of the knowledge explosion and the proliferation of departments, it is even likely that faculty members in adjoining offices are unaware of their mutual contributions. The planning and consultation for retrenchment can be a positive contribution to communication and understanding on campus.

The second major advantage is the exposure each area receives from the external critique. Everyone runs the danger of contracting the bureaucratic disease of having the means become the end. An analysis by outside parties may indicate whether a department's policies and practices are a productive part of the larger whole or are a method of self-protection. It may be extremely helpful to find out which priorities outsiders feel one should be emphasizing. It has been a shock to many offices to find out that the people they served had a completely different set of priorities and expectations for their operation. Each group is going to point somewhere else and ask, why don't we cut that service instead of ours? As noted at the beginning, there are limits to the extent of participation by campus constituencies in retrenchment proceedings. A protectionist attitude on the part of many is to be expected. It is by no means an easy task to channel such attitudes to a constructive role in what has to be a painful exercise at best. At some point, the campus administration must be willing to say that this is the way it is going to be. The responsibility for establishing policies, procedures, timetables, and goals in a period of financial exigency rests ultimately with the president as delegated by the board of governors. The president alone is responsible for the analysis of all of the data and for the final decision.

"Gaming": A Useful Exercise

"Gaming" of the alternatives is an important factor to be considered. "Gaming" is used here to indicate testing of the various proposals and solutions for the immediate and long-range problems of the institution. Unfortunately, any leak of the various courses of action the administration or committees are considering often makes it a fait accompli with all the attendant morale problems for campus employees. Secret or restricted "gaming" allows the testing of even the most outlandish proposals. Beyond that, it also allows the examination of potential consequences of an anticipated action. For instance, a particular proposal may appear acceptable to all parties, but that very action may set the college back several years when affirmative action guidelines are applied. This may be reason enough to drop the proposal from further consideration.

How does the personnel administrator get ready for the "gaming" exercises? The first step is to establish a series of charts, one for every office, service, function and department on the campus. (See Figure 5-1.) Each group should be identified in seniority order on the chart. The appropriate groups would be

Names by Date of Appointment	Budget #	Salary	Sex	Minority
Tenured				
James Jones	153	20,500	M	No
Jane Smith	162	24,300	F	No
Douglas Hoffman	122	25,000	M	No
James Turner	130	23,000	M	No
Untenured				
Susan Acker	1112	18,000	F	Yes
Jeff Pollace	126	17,500	M	No
Paul Gilchrist	172	17,500	M	Yes
Joyce Smith	169	16,500	F	Yes
Judy Griffen	120	16,500	F	No
Part-Time				
Ruth Newton	1126	2,500	F	No
Mildred Green	180	3,000	F	No

Figure 5-1. Example of Departmental Chart for Gaming Exercise.

faculty, administration, management, clerical, and support personnel. Seniority should be established by local policy or, if there is a union contract, by provisions and procedures in the contract. All part-time, temporary, and student employees should also be listed on the same chart by function. Only with these charts in view can management or the consulting committees properly evaluate the direct and peripheral impact of any decisions. Using this method, the effect on affirmative action, education, and worker morale can be programmed and considered. The financial savings and costs can also be determined by inclusion of the salaries and titles of all employees on the charts. Only when this has been accomplished and all alternatives fully explored can top administrators move to adopt a particular plan and begin preparing with confidence for its implementation.

Once the personnel to be excised have been identified, other factors may be considered prior to actual notification of the affected individuals. One prime factor is the effect the personnel actions would have on the institution's affirmative action program. If the impact is going to be too great on minorities and women, the administration or committees may wish to reconsider their programmatic decisions before acting. The fiscal impact is also a factor that clouds the programmatic decisions already made. This would occur when the bottom financial line is added up after all of the personnel actions are decided. One academic program with low FTE production and enrollments could yield $75,000 through the retrenchment of the entire program, an action that may involve only three very senior faculty members. An equal savings through the reduction of clerical help in the academic departments may require the layoff of twelve individuals. Therefore, dollar values and their impact may intrude on the already completed programmatic decisions. An obvious solution would be to consider these factors in the preimplementation stage, but they may not be readily apparent until the program decisions have been completed. Also, it is important to consider what the most important elements of the institution are in various contexts. "Program first and money second" may be the most appropriate priority order, especially when it comes time to justifying the actions of the administration.

Implementation Stage

The implementation stage is the most critical part of the entire retrenchment process. The consequences of any actions taken during this period are most susceptible to review by the courts. Therefore, the local procedure should follow a minimum of four steps: (1) program identification, (2) personnel identification, (3) notification procedures, and (4) follow-up procedures.

Previous discussion has already underlined the importance of identifying the programs to be retrenched through an extensive consultation procedure. However, it is important to emphasize this procedure and its possible impact on the courts if the actions of the institution are challenged. Financial exigency indicates a restriction in the cash flow of an institution. If retrenchment is selected as the method to tighten the institutional belt, then programmatic retreat and consequent personnel reduction is the only acceptable method. If the people are selected first and the institution then rehires other individuals to perform the same tasks, it could be construed as a prima facie case of house cleaning under the guise of financial exigency. There is always a temptation to get rid of the deadwood, but retrenchment under the guise of financial exigency is not the appropriate method.

Personnel identification is the most critical part of the process if conflict with the courts is to be avoided. Since the reason for the personnel excisement is exclusively financial, the institution should be willing to make every effort possible to relocate the affected individuals internally or externally. Institutions may even want to consider a long-range plan of reduction that would involve programmatic adjustments with certain monies set aside for the retraining of faculty members.

If a union contract exists, retrenchment must proceed according to the negotiated layoff procedures. If a contract is not present, layoffs should proceed in the fairest manner possible under the given circumstances.[8] Fairness would dictate that all part-time employees be excised before full-time employees. All nontenured employees should be excised before tenured employees. These steps should be adhered to within the individual retrenchment units identified on a specific campus. The above should not be applied campuswide, since the impact of programs and services would be a matter of chance and detrimental to the long-term health and viability of the institution.

Development of notification procedures is the most personally difficult stage in any layoff. Though every effort should be expended to do it humanely, the individual traumas that will occur are difficult to predict. Therefore, a program of personal assistance should be mandated by each institution facing the difficulties of retrenchment. First, identical formal letters should be sent to all employees to be laid off or retrenched. The letters should be delivered to the employee personally by a top administrative official. Also, the letter should include instructions to the employee for receiving appropriate assistance. Then the personnel office should be charged with the responsibility of providing the following:

1. Documents and advice for obtaining unemployment insurance payments.
2. Information on health and other work-related insurance programs.
3. The names of union officials whom they may wish to consult.
4. An explanation of local, state, or federal rules and regulations that may affect them.
5. Referral to the proper unemployment assistance offices in the immediate area.

6. A list of social service agencies that may be used by the employee.
7. Assistance in the preparation and distribution (not costs) of personal resumes.
8. Initial personal counseling, if available and necessary.
9. A private room on the campus that would have available all possible job listings.
10. Lists of the qualified applicants who have been laid off or retrenched to send to other appropriate institutions.

If there is a union on campus, the union president should be notified of the layoffs simultaneously with employee notifications. However, union officials should only be notified of the numbers of employees to be laid off by category (faculty, clerical, administrative, etc.). *Under no circumstances should the names of the employees to be laid off be released publicly.* The severe trauma of layoff is intensified when the affected employee's friends and relatives find out. Even though management may be accused of covering up or cleaning house when they refuse to release the names, the protection of the employee is more important than the public image of the institution in this particular situation. The employee *alone* should have the right of divulging his or her circumstances.

Finally, the president should issue a public statement to the press and internal governance forums concerning the impact of the retrenchment action and the rationale for it. Internally, the president may also wish to explain how the final determination of retrenchment and layoff units was arrived at. These statements are best issued carefully in writing. The president should avoid defending either the decision or its rationale. Since decisions will be questioned, debate will only be futile. The president made the final decision alone after appropriate consultation, and the president alone will answer for those decisions in the courts. That's why there are presidents.

Postimplementation Stage

After layoffs and retrenchment actions have been completed, the institution must be maintained in some viable manner. This will require the effort and understanding of all remaining employees and management officials. The obvious key to maximum effort and cooperation is communication. Although communication is important in previous stages of the retrenchment process, it takes on increased urgency in this stage. A comprehensive response to that urgency may help prevent further retrenchment.

All administrators and supervisors should be urging their staffs to ask for and need less. This alone can result in substantial future savings in supplies, equipment, and personnel. On the other hand, administrators should not be looking for time study experts to improve efficiency. Educational institutions are not amenable to this type of control except in a few service areas. What is being suggested is moving offices and furniture less, cleaning less, using the telephone to communicate across campus rather than memos, bulk mailing, and personal participation in the saving program. A lessening of expectations will decrease the need for services and increase the feeling of participation by the campus constituencies. Of course there is nothing to prevent the manager with foresight from implementing many of these strategies and procedures *prior to* a fiscal crisis.

The various institutional constituencies should also be closely involved in subsequent long- and short-term planning. The removal of the "we-they" concept and replacing it with "us" will provide a positive benefit for the campus. Faculty and staff who want to be part of the decision-making process should be accommodated even if they are excluded from the final decision. Given the chance, all employees may be willing to cooperate to some degree in a crisis.

All programs and services should be evaluated on a continuing basis. Change on campuses for the immediate future will require both subtraction and addition. The days of "more is better" have passed. Nonproductive programs by any measure will have to be eliminated to make way for the more productive. The faculty will be more likely to agree to changes if they have been involved in both the planning and the evaluations.

There is also a good chance for a change in faculty attitudes in the future if the financial crisis continues. Except for a small elite, the professional job market is quickly ending the era of the nomadic professoriate. More faculty and staff members will soon realize that if they are lucky they will be at their particular institution for a long time, if not forever. This will give them an increasingly stronger interest in their institution. It could, of course, result in more unionism through a quest for job security or more participation in governance. However, it should also result in more interest on their part in the long-term survival of the institution. The budget committee may even move from the least to the most popular governance assembly.

The manager must also be ready to handle the inevitable negative reactions that result from personnel and program reductions. There will be a flood of mail defending this faculty member and that program. There may be union griev- ances, injunctions, and court suits. The manager should not respond directly or emotionally to these attacks. The statement issued during the implementation stage is sufficient explanation of the actions taken. The attorneys will have to defend all actions during injunctive hearings or court proceedings. This is the time for the total administrative team to "hang tough" and stay together without emotion.

A Look to the Future

Accountability, management systems, and budgeting procedures have created a shift from academic administrators to managers. As the visibility of the key administrators has increased, the attention to the myth of "collegiality" has decreased. Increasing state control in the public sector and limited resources in the private sector have forced a sophistication in the decision-making process that is not readily compatible with more traditional governance systems. The collegial process with reasoned debate between faculty and administrators cannot dovetail with the rapid decisions required by ever-changing fiscal and academic crises. These statements are not intended to belittle more traditional procedures, but rather to indicate the increasing degree of responsibility being thrust upon administrators.

All these factors will be important future training and experience requirements for administrators who must cope with the modern crisis. The practical will have to mix with the more traditional. Scholars who wish to participate will have to be adept in the fields of finance, management, personnel, and planning. Increased efficiency and effectiveness will be required from all levels of administration to insure the quality of the academic establishment. There is already increasing pressure for graduate institutions to provide teaching internships within the scholarly requirements of doctoral programs. A similar requirement for administrators will be a natural outgrowth of this trend.

The day of the administrator simply minding the store so that the faculty can "do their thing" is rapidly passing. Managers will continue to move to the forefront of their institutions as conflicts continue. The highly trained technocrats will increase in importance. The obvious danger is that their control of academic programs may increase through the power of fiscal and information controls. Only through long-range planning and active participation by all campus constituencies can good management of the institution, retention of academic quality, and attention to the needs of students be assured.

References

1. Malcolm G. Scully. "The Board of Education and SUNY at an Impasse." *The Chronicle of Higher Education*, 11:14, December 15, 1975, p. 3.

2. *Johnson & University of Wisconsin System* 377 F. Supp 227 (1974).

3. Michael A. Moore. "Defining and Planning for the Steady State." *Educational Record*, Spring 1975, p. 106.

4. Ibid.

5. "1976 Recommended Institutional Regulations on Academic Freedom and Tenure," *AAUP Bulletin*, Summer 1976, pp. 184-191. See also, W. Todd Furniss, "The 1976 AAUP Retrenchment Policy," *Educational Record*, 57:3, Spring 1977, pp. 133-139.

6. Ibid.

7. *Agreement Between the State of New York and United University Professions, Inc.*, 1974-76, pp. 57-60.

8. John C. Tucker. "Financial Exigency—Right, Responsibility and Recent Decision." *The Journal of College and University Law*. 2:2, Winter 74/75.

Introduction to Chapter 6

Will financial exigency be a catalyst to change and innovation in higher education? Or will it force administrators to curtail costly experimentation and foster a return to the basics? One of the most constructive results of the recent period of student activism was renewed interest in finding better ways to conduct educational activities. A whole raft of experiments blossomed forth, from universities without walls to individualized instruction using computers and television. Some were well received; others were not. But change did provide a healthy challenge to traditional ways of doing things.

In this chapter, J. Victor Baldridge, a frequent commentator on academic change and innovation, reviews some of the results of the fiscal crisis that threaten past experimentation. He provides a simple and useful classification system for types of academic change, then investigates how financial exigency is likely to affect each type. Perhaps most significantly, Baldridge offers a number of explicit strategies for administrators to capitalize on fiscal stringency to encourage innovations and changes that promote academic efficiency without sacrificing academic quality.

6

Financial Pressures and Strategies for Higher Education

J. Victor Baldridge

Academic "innovation" is a thing we all hold dear to our hearts. Even if we don't know what we mean by "innovation," it's a Good Thing. And we are all very much afraid that the financial crisis threatening higher education may undermine innovation and change. That threat is the topic of this chapter. We begin with an exploration of some of the general results of the financial crisis, then review more precisely what "innovation" and "change" actually are, what impact growing problems of financial exigency are having on innovation, and conclude with suggested strategies for stimulating and managing constructive changes even in the face of admittedly serious problems.

General Developments Resulting from the Financial Crisis

The financial crisis is having enormous impact on decision making, on the allocation of resources, and on the internal political dynamics of institutions. In turn these will have their impact on innovation and change. We must first examine some of these broad institutional changes before we can say what will happen to change and innovation.

Growth of Faculty Unions

It is fair to say that unions provide employees with a defense mechanism against the economic crisis, the labor market, and other assaults from the external environment. Unfortunately, one of unionism's likely consequences is that institutions will now have less flexibility for changing programs if reductions in personnel result. The rules and regulations of contracts will also make it increasingly difficult for institutions to undertake major shifts in faculty personnel necessary for any significant innovation.

Centralization of Authority

Centralization occurs both at the local campus level and in large systems. There is increased pressure from the legislature and the governor's office for cost reduction in public institutions. These pressures result in a strong centralized

83

attempt to get control over financial matters. Even in private institutions the financial crisis is forcing strong centralization of authority as administrators struggle to promote operating efficiency.

Will centralization hurt innovation or help it? That depends, of course, on the nature of the innovation. Some innovations are best promoted from centralized authorities—for example, establishing a new college or a new management information system. Other innovations are best promoted by decentralized activities—for example, a shift in teaching practices or curriculum. Centralization need not necessarily result in less innovation, but it will be significantly different from a diffuse, decentralized attempt.

Decision Making Is Increasingly "Political"

As resources diminish, various interest groups who see their positions threatened will fight to protect their interests. The level of *conflict* in this political arena seems considerably higher as a result of financial pressure. Thus, any attempt to innovate often faces hostile opposition by people who may feel innovation will be at their expense. The funds for change, for example, may decrease funds needed in other areas. Therefore, the political dynamics of innovation will be highlighted in a period of scarce resources.

Proliferation of Veto Groups

In *The Lonely Crowd*, David Reisman helped spread the idea of "veto groups."[1] It is increasingly difficult for groups to initiate action, but increasingly easy for groups to *stop* action. Anyone who has recently worked in a college or university sees this phenomenon vividly. As procedural regulations become more complicated, and as governance mechanisms involve more and more interest groups, the tendency to block any change is greatly magnified. Essentially, the veto process is a subset of the political process of decision making.

Diminished Student Influence

A few years ago student participation in decision making seemed to be the wave of the future. Today that wave looks more like a ripple. The fresh viewpoints that students brought to the decision-making arena have essentially been stifled. During the sixties, students often were significant proponents and leaders in academic transformations. Today, that pattern is less clear at most institutions, though there are signs that students-as-consumers may generate greater concern for student interests.

In summary, the picture today is considerably more complex. Financial crisis has spawned a variety of defensive strategies including the growth of unions, the exclusion of students, and a growing centralization of decision making. Innovation has become increasingly political as different groups compete for tighter and tighter resources. All this adds up to a situation in which groups can undermine almost any change by exercising a political veto. Truly enormous expenditures of energy have become necessary for any innovation to be sustained.

Given this complex picture, is innovation dead? Are there some redeeming factors that may support innovation during this period? Are we facing a period of rampant conservatism where everybody retrenches and draws back from creative new enterprises? Before we can answer these questions, we must first establish more clearly what we mean by "innovation and change."

Types of Academic Change

Probably more sheer nonsense has been written about the subject of "academic innovation" than anything else. "Innovation" is an emotional word that conjures up images of bright ideas, people doing exciting things, and refreshing winds of change blowing through stagnant institutions: Joe Smith at Circleville U. introducing computers as a teacher of math, Sally Brown at Western College creating a nifty new sociology course using simulation games, Brownville school district holding "innovation and creativity" seminars for its instructors. All through the literature, especially the pop magazine and trade sheets, there is constant fussing about issues of academic innovation and change.

Unfortunately, the vast bulk of the talk and writing about innovation is pretty thin. Practically anything can be an innovation for somebody. Under the rubric of "innovation" we go from the sublime to the ridiculous, from a massive change such as rebuilding the State University of New York at Buffalo to such things as adopting a new "teaching strategy" in a freshman classroom. That is not to say that different kinds of innovations are not interesting, or useful, or good. But it is to say that under this topic there is a great deal of confused, muddled talk.

This is particularly true when a crisis, in this case a massive financial crisis, shakes up the system and calls old assumptions into question. Careers are built on innovation. Bright young men and women have made their way up in the academic world by being innovators. It is a good thing to be an innovator; it is a bad thing to be a "change resistor." It is a good thing to stimulate innovation; it is a bad thing to fight the changes. But in the midst of the financial crisis that now faces higher education, muddled thinking and superficial discussions of innovations can get us into trouble.

To clear the air somewhat about terminology I would like to suggest three major types of academic change, each with several subcategories.

Fundamental Institutional Change

The most fundamental kind of innovation is a shift in institutional mission or objectives. This is a massive change, a change that really makes a difference. In the last decade we have seen many examples of such sweeping institutional change. First, there is a total reorientation of existing institutions or the creation of an entirely new institution. The creation of the Open University in England is probably one of the best illustrations. The spawning of hundreds of new community colleges in the United States is also a classic case.

In addition, there have been substantial changes in existing institutions. SUNY at Buffalo is a substantially different institution than it was ten years ago. NYU has significantly changed its mission over the last decade. The City College of New York has spawned bold new initiatives in open admissions and minority recruitment only to have them partially crushed by the financial disaster in New York. There are many other cases of truly massive institutional change: Antioch College's exciting experiments, the attempt to set up "nontraditional" colleges at Governor's State, Evergreen State, Empire State, and others. There are several important pieces of literature about fundamental institutional change. Warren Bennis wrote a fascinating article on the transformation of the University of Buffalo called, "Who Sank the Yellow Submarine?"[2] Baldridge wrote a book on the transformation of NYU.[3] Burton R. Clark produced an important piece on major institutional changes at Reed, Swarthmore, and Antioch.[4]

Intermediate Changes

The second type of basic institutional change is somewhat less dramatic, but quite common nevertheless. This is the creation of major new thrusts within subunits of an institution, such as starting a new medical school, a new school of engineering, or a new minorities study center. During the last decade many internal institutional changes have had major impact. The creation of urban study centers at many major universities is an excellent example.

There are three types of intermediate level change. First, there are *major curriculum revisions*. The introduction of a new general education requirement for a whole institution is an example. The creation of new "cluster colleges" such as at Santa Cruz and the University of Michigan are cases in point.

Second, innovations in *student life* and *student housing* have often been significant. In the past decade many campuses made exciting attempts to improve student life in the face of growing bureaucracy and increased institutional size. The development of cluster colleges, the introduction of living and learning strategies into residence halls, and the inclusion of students in campus senates are all good examples of this kind of change. Many of these changes have significant impact on the learning and living styles of students.

Finally, there are changes in *administrative arrangements*. Shifts in administrative style have been rather pronounced in the last decade. Particularly important, of course, has been a centralization of authority in state systems. In addition, on local campuses there have been attempts to introduce "new management practices," attempts to cut costs and to develop sophisticated information systems. For example, over the past four years, the Exxon Educational Foundation funded forty-three private liberal arts colleges with grants to introduce improved management practices.

Small-Scale Changes

The massive institutional changes are probably the least common. The intermediate-level changes are somewhat more frequent. But the most widespread changes often discussed in the literature, are fairly small-scale shifts in curriculum, class activities, and instructional techniques. "Small-scale" simply means that few people are involved in each particular incidence of change. The *cumulative* effect of large numbers of these individual changes, though, may be substantial. Most of the literature that deals with "innovation" in educational organizations deals with these small-scale changes. Thus, we can find numerous reports on new class activities, team teaching, and the use of sophisticated television media for class instruction.[5]

Again, while there is no easy way to classify all of these changes, they can be roughly divided into two classes. First, there are changes in *classroom activities* such as team teaching, the use of simulation games, and the use of new curriculum materials. Incidentally, many of these changes result from new products produced by publishing houses. The role of the publishing industry in promoting educational change has rarely been examined but probably is quite significant.

A second change that is growing in popularity is the *use of media for teaching*. The experiments in this area are widespread. Unfortunately the results are mixed at best. It is fair to say that Americans are enamored with hardware, but by comparison to the British Open University, they have done a pathetic job in developing good programming. An official of the British Open University recently commented, "A dull, stuffy and uninteresting lecture put on color TV with stereophonic sound is still a basically dull, stuffy and uninteresting lecture. And that is the major failure of American attempts at using the mass media."[6] In spite of its problems, the introduction of media as a teaching tool is still an important educational innovation.

We could elaborate on the three-stage taxonomy of educational change described in this section, but this rough version should suffice here. Unfortunately, there is a good deal of confusion about educational innovation, and it would help if people would clarify what they mean when they talk about it. The task here is not to build an elaborate classification. The point is to make some distinctions that will now be used to discuss the impact of the financial crisis.

The Impact of the Financial Crisis

The sixties were boom times, and the seventies are looking increasingly leaner. Colleges are closing their doors, tightening their belts, foregoing pay raises, struggling with declining enrollments, and hassling with state legislatures. The question is, *What will the financial crisis do to strategies of innovation and change in higher education?* Will the financial crisis undermine some of the fresher ideas of the sixties? Will the scramble to consolidate and retrench snuff out attempts to develop new educational strategies? Will the defensive reactions of faculty, as best exemplified in the growth of unionism, be a conservative force? Conventional wisdom holds that the financial crisis can seriously undermine the thrust for change and innovation.

We must, however, be more discriminating than to assume that hard times will stifle effective change wherever change is proposed. For one thing, nothing *promotes* internal change as much as strong external pressures threatening institutional survival. In his recent study of over 100 institutions where innovations had been attempted, Mayhew found that one potent triggering force for innovation and change was financial exigency.[7] By itself, of course, financial exigency does not guarantee that effective change will occur or be sustained. But it does present an opportunity that skilled leadership can use to advance innovation and change. Given the nature of financial exigency, we can probably assume that where this threat is clearly perceived, change is likely to be institutional in scope. This is so because rising costs and declining enrollments threaten the very survival of the institution. However, only relatively few institutions have yet experienced the kind of trauma necessary to galvanize the entire campus community to action, and by then it may be too late.

For most institutions, the dictates of conventional wisdom are probably right. Rather than perceive growing austerity as an opportunity to be seized, most individuals and institutions "pull in their horns." Crisis always brings a sense of fear, and a sense of fear usually generates a deeply entrenched conservatism. The Great Depression of the 1930s left an indelible mark on the people of that era. The depression of higher education seems to be leaving the same kind of conservative mark on academic institutions today. There is a hesitancy to innovate and a drive toward consolidation rather than expansion. Innovation and academic creativity may be substantially stifled for the next few years as a consequence.

Intermediate and Smaller Scale Innovation Continues

During the sixties much of the excitement in higher education was due to truly large-scale changes. The number of community colleges increased at a fantastic rate. The City University of New York plunged into a variety of dynamic and exciting experiments, virtually transforming its institutional mission. The State University of New York was born of a collection of teachers' colleges and small four-year colleges. The impressive centers at Buffalo and Stonybrook were formed. In California the state college and university system was set up. Enrollments increased, programs proliferated, and massive institutional changes occurred. The onset of the steady-state enrollment and the arrival of the financial crisis has abruptly stopped most massive changes.

It is harder to judge what has happened to intermediate and small-scale changes. Their effects on the national scene are not so obvious and it takes considerable guesswork to say anything about them. However, I would venture to guess that intermediate and small-scale changes have also decreased slightly. But the shift is not all in the direction of less innovation. For example, in the intermediate area, administrative changes have probably increased rather than decreased. More new strategies are available for information gathering, computer processing, and modern decision techniques. When the financial crisis arrived many institutions quickly adopted the new processes. Also some major curriculum shifts are probably occurring, almost as a reaction against many of the new ideas developed in the sixties. Whether this is innovation or whether it is rampant conservatism is open to debate.

For small-scale changes the general level of innovation has probably decreased somewhat simply because money is less available. However, this area is probably constantly changing and is likely to be a source of continued innovation in higher education. New classroom activities will be produced in spite of budget cutbacks, and media may even be more extensively used to cut costs.

In short, we are probably seeing a fairly radical shift in the *type* of innovation. The massive large-scale changes of institutional goals through deliberate planning has probably decreased. In fact, many retrenchments of personnel and program may be caused by drastic financial pressure. The intermediate changes are probably reduced, but there are nevertheless many new administrative experiments to cope with the financial crisis. And the small-scale changes will probably continue even if at a reduced level.

Overall Innovation Activity Has Decreased

Not only has the *type* of innovation changed but the general *level* of innovative activity has probably decreased. The obvious answer is that money is not available. As faculties have been cut back and student enrollments have leveled off there seems to be a period of rampant traditionalism, consolidation, status quo thinking, and even significant retrenchment. Organization theorists generally argue that organizations innovate when there is sufficient "slack resources," that is, when there is enough free money to do new things. There are few slack resources in higher education at the moment. The classic and obvious case is the retrenchment at City University of New York. Not only are the so-called frills being eliminated, but the very heart of the institutional mission is being attacked. We cannot argue away or dismiss the fact that institutional innovation is being stifled as a result of the financial crisis.

The Application of Traditional Standards and Criteria

The sixties saw many interesting experiments. The seventies are seeing a lot of backing and filling. Money gets tight, people try to hang on to jobs, and the old traditional criteria of publishing and teaching are looming even larger. People who were "innovators" a few years ago are now "frill experts." Young professors who spent a lot of time spawning exciting ideas in the late sixties are now frantically publishing articles to make tenure in the seventies. In the grim market for Ph.D.'s most institutions have responded by implementing very traditional measures of quality. Why have a bright young person who is making his or her way on "innovative" activities when you can substitute a Ph.D. from Berkeley who publishes in important and learned journals? When you have an oversupply of Ph.D.'s you can demand higher "quality"—a quality measured in absolutely traditionalistic terms. A wave of rampant traditionalism has infected various areas of the country in the last couple of years. Of course, administrators and promotion committees will argue they are simply getting "better" people. The net result, however, is that they are also getting fairly traditional people who are willing to follow the ancient party lines concerning academic performance. The traditional academic reward system is having an added impact.

How Can We Act Creatively in the Face of These Pressures?

To argue that innovation and creativity can flourish in the face of all the counterpressures is to argue unrealistically. We are simply in for a period of belt tightening. Nevertheless, a few comments about ways of supporting changes and innovation even in these bad times are appropriate. The following is a set of rules, a set of strategies for supporting change and fostering creativity. These ideas will not solve the problem—but they will give us something to do while we ride out the storm!

Innovate by Cutting Back

Frankly, the financial crisis allows us to be innovative in many institutions by cutting out the deadwood. We normally conceive of innovation as *adding* new activities. After a decade of considerable expansion many institutions could more adequately serve their students by taking a serious look at what they are doing, cutting off some of the frills and excesses, and concentrating on some central issues. *Basically, the decision about what is needed must be based on better response to student and community needs.* The students in this era are asking for different things than they were several years ago. There is a renewed awakening in career education, in job preparation, and in many traditional subjects. The forces in the sixties were in the opposite direction, and we now may find that we can better serve our students by trimming back on some of the things we did during the sixties. This may not sound like a particularly exciting way to innovate, but if the criteria is student service, it is possible.

Concentrate Efforts on High Impact Projects

In the past decade administrators, faculty, and students alike could attack a wide variety of issues and propose a broad spectrum of innovations. The money was plentiful, the institutions were expanding, and the opportunities for innovation were abundant. Today, however, the picture is obviously different. We cannot afford to support everything. It makes more sense to be extremely careful about selecting high-impact, serious programs. We cannot afford to run in many different directions at the same time. The resources are simply not generous enough for this kind of diffuse activity. As a consequence, anyone wanting to innovate in today's environment probably should select a basic target and make a concentrated effort in that direction.

One powerful strategy that has rarely been used is to conduct planned experiments. Innovations in higher education rarely offer opportunities to measure different outcomes from different processes. That is, if we focus on a problem such as poor writing skills in freshmen students it would be sensible to try four or five alternative approaches at the same time. A comparison of the alternative approaches would be much more valuable than the standard practice of having *one* approach that has no comparative reference. This kind of experiment is remarkably rare considering that almost all the social sciences explicitly call for experimental controls in their research. Organizational changes are rarely conducted with a serious experimental and evaluation design. Concentrating on a few important issues, with deliberate planned experimental variations, may have higher payoff than scattering our efforts over many issues.

Promise Only What Can Be Delivered

More than ever it is important to have reasonable expectations about what can and cannot happen. In the sixties we could promise the moon—and surprisingly enough we often could deliver it (or an acceptable facsimile). In the seventies our promises must be consistent with the available resources. Nothing generates frustration, hostility, and low morale more than promises unfulfilled. It seems wise to lower our expectations, to make promises we can keep, and to concentrate on incremental reforms rather than sweeping big plans. It is interesting that Governor Jerry Brown of California has made his political career on the premise that "less is more," that he will deliver public services in line with public abilities to pay. Whether one agrees with Jerry Brown's politics is immaterial. His basic point is probably sensible for higher education in contemporary society.

Greater Impetus from Central Authorities

This applies on both the local campus and large systems. In a financial crisis much authority flows to central administrations. The logical consequence is that central administrations will have to be a prime catalyst for change. More than ever, success or failure of an academic innovation will depend on support from the central administration. Central administrators should realize this and give support on important issues.

The call for central administrators to be the agents of academic change frankly runs counter to much of the ideology in the field of innovation. The general assumption is always that decentralization is good, that getting the changes made by lower ranks of faculty and students is better, and that widespread "participation" is healthy in order to accomplish change. These may be good assumptions when the resources are plentiful enough that decentralized change is possible. Nevertheless, these assumptions are greatly strained when authority is centralized as a consequence of financial problems. No model is good under all circumstances. The decentralized model works sometimes, but when the decision power is centralized, then the impetus for real change is often centralized. This is a fact regardless of the ultimate impact. Consequently, in today's environment the initiative of top administrators is a key factor in getting major changes.

Marshall Political Support

Where political dynamics are heightened, where the conflict is more evident, and where veto groups are proliferating, the obvious strategy is to play the political factor and marshall political support. The change agent must have the skills of a successful politician, a statesman who can create a supportive interest group around change. Most changes are failures. And much of the explanation is that the change supporters are so often inept at the political problems. Interest groups have different concerns. In a period of financial crisis, there will be strong opposition to changes that take money out of one function and put it in another. And almost any change of consequence does exactly that!

To be a successful change agent is to be a successful politician. It is critical to marshall the support of diverse constituencies, to form hard-nosed interest groups who are willing to articulate their plans. However, forming new groups is not the only answer. There are always powerful entrenched blocs of people who must be brought along if any change is to be successful. Most revolutions—and most academic changes—fail because the revolutionaries fail to realize that they have to bring some traditionalists along with them. Political artistry and political savvy are keys to successful academic innovation today. Mayhew notes that successful innovators must become personally, professionally, and emotionally involved with an innovation to assure its adoption and institutionalization. These persons are usually not members of the tenured faculty or entrenched administration. Rather they are on the periphery, commanding respect but independent enough to challenge dominant values and traditional practices. However, Mayhew adds, "Once such a marginal individual begins an innovation he or she must obtain continuing satisfactions from the activity or else the pressures of resistance will prove irresistible and continuation of the activity will not seem worth the effort."[8]

If no internal change agents are readily available, outside consultants can perform this function. But there must be an organizationally supported committee or task force to see that proposed changes and innovations do indeed occur. All too often, promising starts collapse when there is no commitment to sustained effort. Indeed, a carefully selected task force or unit could combine the varied roles of change agent, monitor, and evaluator.

Regardless of which person or group becomes responsible for stimulating or designing innovations, without strong commitment from the president and the administration, the chances for meaningful, sustained change are slim.

Provide the Resources

It is remarkable how many faculty members, department heads, and administrators talk about major changes but are not willing to commit necessary resources. Most of us have heard speeches by administrators calling for new ideas and new creativity—only to find that those same administrators cannot seem to find a nickel to support that creativity. If major changes are seriously desired, some other priorities are going to have to suffer diminished support. That fact is brutal, that fact is simple, and that fact is true in a time of financial exigency. Incidentally, this is another reason why it is so important to line up the political aspects of innovation. "Hard money" must come from another function. And unless the political support exists for shifting priorities, visions of change will remain simply unfulfilled visions.

Institutionalize Change and Innovation

Change is going to be increasingly difficult. The support of change will need all the allies it can get. Large organizations always have a habit of building institutional structures around priorities that they really feel are important. One can almost always tell what an institution's *real* priorities are—as opposed to its verbal priorities—by asking where the money is spent and how the organization is structured. The real priorities will have money and the organization will have formed structural support around them.

Every organization needs a vice-president in charge of change and innovation. This is probably true now more than ever before. If decentralized opportunities for innovation are decreased and centralized authorities hold more and more of the power, then a central official in charge of new strategies is critical. An institution that is serious about not getting bogged down in traditionalism will put aside some money and some people continually to question the system.

This means *senior* staff have to be assigned to the job. There was a time when bright young people often played the role of change catalysts. Today, with the encroaching traditionalism and the return to traditional standards for evaluating faculty, it is simply no longer possible for the bright young people to carry the burden. Some senior staff members who have already passed the tests and already have their power bases established must carry the ball in today's environment. To give the job to junior people is to condemn them to academic death. In short, there must be structural support, generous money, and senior staff if the organization is to support change.

Summary

This chapter has presented a relatively pessimistic picture. The financial crisis is bringing a whole set of new problems to higher education. First, there is a change in some of the fundamental decision processes that govern the institutions. Unions have grown up and are defending the faculty against environmental threats. Authority is being centralized, both on the local campuses and at the state level. Innovation is increasingly political, and there is a proliferation of veto groups that can curtail new activities. Students have been pushed out of the decision processes and their fresh ideas have been largely eliminated, though there are signs of increasing restlessness with ever-increasing tuition and fees, fewer courses, and self-interested faculty members and administrators.

As a consequence, the general level of change and innovation has generally decreased. Traditionalism, consolidation, and retrenchment are the order of the day. This is particularly true of innovations classified as fundamental institutional changes. The intermediate changes and the small-scale changes may actually find themselves increasing under certain circumstances. But change now fights an uphill battle against a new traditionalism and a new application of old quality standards.

While the picture is grim, it need not be hopeless. In some ways, the financial crisis has offered us a healthy chance to trim down after the fantastic growth of the past decade. The opportunities for change, although very difficult, are nevertheless still possible. Certain strategies seem to be more helpful at this time than others. Concentration of effort is important, with basic targets being selected for planned experimentation. Central authorities will play a greater role as both the impetus for change and the support for change.

It is important to stress the essentially political character of the change process. Veto groups abound, conflict is high, resources are scarce, and the battles are vicious. However, if we can strive for changes that are reasonable, and if we promise only what we can deliver, we may find that academic change is possible even in the face of enormous difficulties. But it will not be easy.

References

1. David Riesman. *The Lonely Crowd.* New Haven: Yale University Press, 1950.

2. Warren Bennis. "Who Sank the Yellow Submarine?" *Psychology Today*, November 1972.

3. J. Victor Baldridge. *Power and Conflict in the University.* New York: Wiley, 1971.

4. Burton R. Clark. *The Distinctive College.* Chicago: Aldine, 1970.

5. J. Victor Baldridge and Terrence E. Deal. *Managing Change in Educational Institutions.* San Francisco: McCutchan, 1975.

6. Interview with J. Victor Baldridge.

7. Lewis B. Mayhew. *How Colleges Change: Approaches to Academic Reform.* ERIC Clearinghouse for Higher Education, Stanford University, July 1976.

8. Ibid., p. 15.

Introduction to Chapter 7

The social crisis of the sixties and the fiscal crisis of the seventies have forced higher education into a more active role in the political arena. However, the political arena is a dangerous place for a novice. George Angell points out that administrators have traditionally been reluctant to involve themselves with legislators. But the time has passed for remaining remote because major decisions affecting both public and private education are increasingly being made by public officials at all levels of government.

Angell places particular emphasis on the role of the campus president in the political setting, noting at the same time that there are serious obstacles to overcome. He presents a convincing case for involvement and suggests that the first order of business is developing a rationale for political action, followed by careful preparation and planning. Drawing on his long experience as a former campus president and as the director of a national organization where activities relate in part to the legislative arena, Angell devotes considerable space to providing practical advice. Administrators will find in this chapter a detailed description of how to organize both personnel and institutional resources on a step-by-step basis for political action. For educators seeking to make their voices heard in places where major decisions affecting their institutions are likely to be made, this chapter will be indispensable.

7

Entering the Legislative Arena

George W. Angell

In a sense state legislatures have become the great new American melting pot that slowly sifts and sorts the dreams of people, measures them by the yardstick of public opinion, reduces them to the minimal necessities of human need, and funds only those that will help win reelections. If this sounds negative it is not meant to be. It is an ordinary response of reasonable people to a long period of public overassurance, overspending, underplanning, and unreasonable expectations. Such a period was 1945 to 1975 in America. It took Vietnam, Sputnik, inflation, unemployment, an oil shortage, and Watergate to raise doubts and initiate more realistic thoughts. More than anything else the specter of another Great Depression struck fear in the hearts of America, and fear can change the political scene. For the first time in thirty years, legislators in the seventies cut existing social welfare programs and generally refused to consider any new programs that cost money, not matter how humane, decent, and essential they may have seemed to their partisans.

In turn, the natural reaction to legislative intransigence is the organization of power blocs capable of overriding the fears and sometimes the sound judgment of legislators. Strong environmental groups have sprung up throughout the nation. State and national student lobbies have almost overnight gained unexpected legislative respect and influence. State and national unions of teachers have recently gained political powers of unprecedented magnitude. Coalitions of oil lobbies have blunted the march of the environmentalists. Chambers of Commerce and tax reform groups have redoubled their efforts to cut public expenditures. Confederations of city, village, and county governments have become especially effective in fighting for more state aid to local governments and school districts.

But who is fighting in the state legislatures for higher education? The answer is, almost no one. At least no one with political clout. College presidents and trustees for the most part are unwilling to be drawn into power struggles and prefer to remain aloof from the tough political in-fighting that today characterizes the passage of every piece of significant legislation. There are those wonderful rare exceptions, of course, to whom higher education owes its existence and residual vitality. But the number is hardly equal to the task of addressing the many issues currently affecting higher education. Table 7-1 lists some of the more important decisions to be decided largely in the political arena. Each may appear relatively benign but their collective significance is awesome.

Table 7-1
Decisions about Higher Education Made at Different Levels of Government

Local Government	State Government	Federal Government
Support of academic freedom	Collective bargaining legislation	Affirmative action
Support of lifelong learning program	Budgetary support for public colleges and universities	Privacy regulations
Financial support (especially for community colleges)	Financial aid to public and private colleges and universities	Federal enforcement of civil rights legislation
Tax exemptions	Budgeting and auditing controls	Federal safety and health legislation
Cooperative public service programs	Budgeting and auditing controls over campus personnel decisions	Federal program support
Tax base issues	Role of courts and labor boards in settling campus disputes	Student financial aid
Form of control	Scope of bargaining	Institutional aid (e.g., capital construction)
Appointment of trustees	Appointment of trustees	Judicial/regulatory agency involvement
Regulations related to student conduct	Statewide financial aid to students	Consumer legislation
Public utilities and services (cost of power, police and fire protection, health and sanitation services, etc.)	Autonomy of colleges and universities in relation to central coordinating agencies	Research support
Traffic regulation	Relationship with other state agencies	Extension of Wagner Act to states and subdivisions
Zoning	Public service programs	Tax exemptions (especially for philanthropic giving)
Transportation expenditures (streets, airport, by-passes)	Support of university research	Status of educational foundations
Attitude of courts toward students	Role of trustees in university governance	
	Tenure, academic freedom, etc.	
	Retirement programs	

Events of the seventies have proven that colleges and universities are politically impotent. Twenty-four states have passed collective bargaining laws[1] about which college officials knew very little or upon which they had little or no influence. At the federal level, the Higher Education Amendments of 1972 were passed based on fundamental concepts widely differing with those held generally by the higher education community.[2] Yet these laws have the most serious political and operational effects on public colleges and universities as well as upon private higher education. Faculty unions bypass presidents to go to governing boards or to governors to overrule trustees and chancellors.[3] Administrative positions have been eliminated, downgraded, and underfunded. Colleges, divisions, and programs are retrenched; yet student enrollments grow in some areas. Public college leaders fight other public colleges for funds and programs. Public and private colleges put on a friendly cooperative front, but behind closed legislative doors personal survival triumphs. Student lobbies fight for lower tuition and fees while faculty lobbies fight for higher salaries and more fringe benefits.

The way in which colleges and universities have been literally shoved around by state and federal agencies purporting to represent justice and affirmative action has, to some observers, made higher education and its devotion to "excellence" look ridiculous. And higher education representatives will continue to look more and more like political puppets until they develop unity, direction, and political sophistication.

Role of Campus Presidents in the Legislative Arena

To enter the political arena successfully, a college executive has to be motivated by an unshakable faith in the ultimate goodness of what he or she constantly professes: that a strong, inexpensive, higher education is essential to a free and humane society. A college executive must believe that every dollar for higher education obtained from governments, foundations, and other donors is the finest possible investment the human community can make on behalf of its own future. Lacking this source of energy there is no human fiber to withstand the rebuffs of politicians and the accusations of competitors.

Today's college president must also be motivated by a realization that higher education is and always will be only one of many worthy competitors for public support. Since there are fewer and fewer other sources of substantial support, the future of higher education, public and private, depends upon the political competence of its leaders.

Purpose and Political Action

Since political activity always carries a high degree of risk, one must ask, why take the chance? The answer is, of course, to achieve purposes that cannot be achieved outside the political arena. What are those purposes? Peculiarly enough, the primary purpose is freedom from political dominance and interference. Unfortunately, our republican form of government, at least during the twentieth century, is itself the prisoner of powerful special interests. During the growth period of the sixties, almost all colleges were the recipients of huge sums of largess from governments and private donors. This heady experience has created ties of friendship and dependence that must not become chains of bondage. Lewis Perelman put it this way: "In the first academic revolution [1960s] the economic system clearly led the higher education system. In the second academic revolution . . . the higher education system must take the responsibility of leading the economic system. To follow is to pursue crisis and to court disaster."[4]

A second purpose is equally important: to free the institution from faculty dominance and to create a new unity among university constituents. Collective bargaining has created a direct alliance between faculty and organized labor. The resulting political clout is already being felt during elections and the passage of legislation. It was a coalition of educational and public employee unions that put into the 1976 National Democratic platform a plank supporting federal legislation on regulations giving public employees (faculty in public colleges and universities) the right to unionize and bargain. It is the faculty unions in New York, Pennsylvania, and New Jersey that deal directly with their respective governor's offices to determine salaries, benefits, promotions, research, merit awards, and other campus policies while bypassing campus presidents and trustees. Such a process can and has placed colleges and universities under the dominance of political processes to which institutional leadership has been virtually denied meaningful access.[5]

Universities under the dominance of faculties and governors are directed toward security and mediocrity, not excellence. Unions and governors are never fired because a university is mediocre. Presidents are. Yet presidents and trustees are losing their power to take decisive action. This is not to deny the positive contributions of unions. They are born of necessity and are pursuing valid goals. Faculty unions are begging for help from strong institutional leadership, but find little. In the Pennsylvania colleges, it was the faculty unions who fought for individual campus autonomy. It was the presidents who succumbed to political pressure from the lieutenant governor and submitted to centralized statewide bargaining.

Obstacles to Overcome

If the first step is to know one's weaknesses, the second surely is to know the character and magnitude of the obstacles to be overcome. A quick rundown of some common problems faced by campus executives inexperienced in state political life may be helpful.

First, campus executives are generally afraid of regional politicians and of creating antagonisms not only among legislators but among faculty, trustees, state departments (especially the governor's budget office), and state boards of higher education. Such fears are only well founded where obtuse, uncivil, unannounced, and poorly planned methods are used. Legislators, budget officers, and administrative superiors not only respect but admire campus executives who fearlessly and in good humor do their job well. (In fact they often try to employ them.)

Second, few campus presidents place a high priority on political leadership. For one thing, campus presidents still think they are "curriculum creators." Most of them, brought up from academic teaching ranks, have little experience in organizing a complex educational institution; as a result, they spend most of their time trying to mediate disputes among internal power blocs of faculty departments, student groups, and community interests. In addition, too many government offices want to change the university's budgeting, accounting, and long-range planning procedures every year without giving the last approach a chance to prove its value. And to add insult to injury, there are simply too many *new* government requests and demands (such as Title IX) that overburden campuses because those same governments usually fail to provide funds for additional campus personnel, sensible guidelines, and data retrieval capability to meet the new compliance demands. Finally, the courts themselves have in one decade gone too far too fast in trying to determine whether or not an academic community must be operated precisely as a civil community. In summary, college and university executives have very little time to do anything except to try to meet crises thrust upon them by people over whom they exercise little control.

Third, few chancellors of public higher educational systems are well suited to their political jobs. Yet they have vast authority over many campuses. They are usually located in the state's capitol, the center of political action, and are subject to daily political pressures. Still they see their jobs primarily as being academic leaders. What they are loathe to admit is that, in fact, their opportunity to serve the higher education community of the state is primarily political. Since they have little heart, experience, or desire for political involvement it is not difficult for politicians and unions to perceive and take advantage of this obvious political weakness. Of course, no one (except perhaps faculty unions) will publicly admit to this, but any legislative assistant can verify that this is occurring much more frequently in 1976 than in 1966 or in 1956. Herein, perhaps, lies the campus executive's chief obstacle to political effectiveness: his administrative superior may be politically ineffective.

Fourth, presidents misconceive the role of the state office of higher education and their own relationship to it. They expect the chief state educational officer to be their political leader, when, in fact, he or she is, too often, a prisoner of the state's political system. Only the campus presidents, determined and united, unafraid and active, can provide the grass roots (precinct) political leadership from which state educational power is fashioned.

The fifth obstacle, and perhaps the one of most importance, is that there is simply too much conflict within higher education to provide a strong political base. Each institution believes it should "have the most" and be "the best." That is only natural. But to carry on the tradition of superficial cooperation is childish. United, higher education has some chance to survive and even renew itself in a politically dominated society.

The sixth obstacle is the lack of a united educational leadership at the national level. Well-meaning, highly intelligent, hard-working professionals staff the national offices of higher education. But they are woefully undermanned and often are given misdirection by well-meaning but unsophisticated members of their boards.

Preparation for Political Action

Rationale

A campus executive can gain considerable courage and motivation by developing a sound rationale for moving into the political arena. It is fundamental to believe, after due consideration, that it is not only the best direction in which to move, but that there is no feasible alternative for securing the financial and legal base upon which to build the institution's future. Convinced of this the executive should study carefully the potential negative as well as positive outcomes from one's personal political involvement. One possible outcome, of course, is summary dismissal with no due process mechanism available for defense. A campus executive of a public institution is, from a political viewpoint, a member of the state executive hierarchy which takes orders from the governor. Political activity inconsistent with a superior's orders may be considered insubordinate and grounds for dismissal. If one's superiors are so insecure as to prohibit any significant political activity, the way is more precarious, but nevertheless, still open and worth consideration. Although the position of the private college executive is less directly threatened, he or she is not exempt from similar problems of insubordination to the governor's wishes.

A second point of rationale is to recognize the legal mandates and responsibilities requiring a campus executive to provide public information about the condition and needs of the institution and, when needed, to request public assistance in improving them. The campus president cannot avoid the duty to express publicly his concern (a "political" action) relative to the needs of his institution when it may be interpreted as an act of insubordination by his superior. Persuaded of this duty the executive simply chooses among alternative *methods* of publicizing institutional needs.

A third point of rationale is that the executive must feel the necessity to use every opportunity possible to declare his political rights as a citizen. Supposedly the executive has the same constitutional rights as others, and in fact, the responsibilities of the office demand that these rights be fully exercised to protect and inform the citizenry. Every time one publicly espouses freedom for oneself as well as for others, it reinforces the determination and desire to be a living example of those didactics. If the administrator speaks in an intelligent and inspirational manner, without threat or pomposity, the politician will seek him as an ally and superiors are likely to appoint him to committees that give him further opportunities to exercise in a wise and timely fashion his newfound "political power." A word of caution: One Pennsylvania college president recently found himself summarily removed from his office, partly because of continued exercise of free speech and action that his superiors deemed to be unwise and insubordinate. Nonetheless, the wise exercise of political privilege (freedom) builds personal political power. Without this personal power of established leadership, a campus executive cannot hope to build *institutional* political effectiveness.

One more cornerstone in the structure of rationale may be worth noting. In a growing number of states (Nebraska, Iowa, Massachusetts, Connecticut, New Jersey, Minnesota, to name a few) political battles are raging, though some are still being fought behind the scenes, about whether the governor or the legislature can overcome constitutional or traditional prohibition of political control of the state's most prestigious public institutions of higher learning. Three major events since 1965 have given politicians new hope for political control: (1) the public's dismay over the abuse of freedom by some university students and faculty members during the late sixties and early seventies; (2) the threat of fiscal bankruptcy unless the expenditures of all state agencies, including universities, are better managed and controlled; and (3) the examples of some states, such as New Jersey and New York, that have usurped the powers of educational trustees by negotiating costs and policies directly with faculty and civil service employee unions. This last factor is the most potent since it has the full support of unions and almost totally escapes enlightened public scrutiny. People in general simply do not understand that political officials, through collective bargaining, are gaining more and more control over the character and purpose of higher education and simultaneously are reducing the capacity and flexibility of institutions to change and meet the needs of new generations of students for different kinds of education.

Unfortunately, only a handful of college presidents and trustees understand fully the impact of faculty collective bargaining. Those who do have little difficulty finding the courage to speak out. But again, unfortunately, they often speak out about the wrong issues (e.g., "faculty should not have the right to bargain"; "unions are dangerous"; "unions don't care about the institution") and in the process lose rather than gain political influence. This leads directly then to the first step in organizing for political action, that of setting one's own institution "in order."

Knowing One's Institution

The most significant ingredient of success in the political arena is knowledge. Knowledge that permits not only easy and factual response to wide-ranging questions, but also insight that extends the politician's and public's interest to questions not ordinarily asked. The campus executive must gear up the institution's machinery to crank out long- and short-range information which is the most effective ammunition in political warfare. Other chapters provide detailed descriptions of several different types of essential information retrieval. For purposes of this chapter, I shall simply outline those types of data essential to the function of political statemanship. First is *cost accounting.* Here the spokesman must know the cost of basic unit expenditures. How much does it cost to produce a graduate nurse? a unit of freshman biology? the admission of one student? What percentage is paid from tax funds? what percentage for administration?

The second is *cost budgeting.* This is the science of building and defending budget requests on the facts of current and projected unit costs.

The third is *cost allocation.* This is the art of making allocations within the institution based on current unit costs, changes in enrollment patterns, past cost-benefit analysis, changing patterns of faculty staffing, and the subvention of promising innovation and research. Without goal-oriented, scientifically balanced allocation of funds by program, no executive can feel comfortable about the vitality of his institution and the proper use of funds already available.

The fourth is *cost-benefit analysis.* Useful cost-benefit studies take at least six to ten years because they include analysis of the aspirations and potential of arriving students, those of graduating students, and the realizations of alumni. Until the "arriving students" actually become alumni with some experience and realization of benefits, the studies lack longitudinal data and the results must be handled gingerly. Nevertheless, any appropriate studies of institutional outcomes are valuable both for better management and more effective political action.

The fifth dimension of orderly administration is *cost-investment.* This is the science and art of selecting and subsidizing educational experimentation and innovation that have the greatest potential for producing short- and long-range benefits. Successful innovation produces immediate faculty and student enthusiasm and release of energy. This leads to immediate news releases that may be beneficial in the political arena, both for gaining respect and additional funding.

Obviously educational as well as any other type of leadership requires the planning and expenditure of *risk capital*—simply speaking, money allocated to support innovation. Innovation, of course, takes many forms including a new program, a new administrative office such as an ombudsman, a series of visiting distinguished professors, establishment of distinguished teaching awards, etc. Perhaps only 10 to 20 percent of a university's attempts at innovation are truly successful. But without careful planning for innovation, little takes place, and rigor mortis sets in.

The last dimension of orderly administration for purposes of this chapter is *cost planning*. Each academic and administrative department of an institution, for stability and vitality, needs to prepare, review, and amend long- and short-range "variable" plans for personnel needs and expenditures. By "variable," I mean that each department should have a series of flexible plans based on a variety of potential conditions. As an example, if enrollments go up 5 percent, how will staffing be affected, if at all? If they go down 5 percent will it be necessary to retrench, and to what extent? How can this be modified by retirements, turnover, and other staffing factors? It is not difficult to see the political overtones of such planning, both internal and external, to the campus. The campus executive who can say to anyone, but especially to legislators and budget directors, that each department has cooperatively made such plans three to eight years in advance should certainly enjoy more public respect and fewer "political" crises than one who cannot. But, finally, one gains confidence and makes better decisions because the facts are available and are used in a systematic and humane fashion becoming an academic community, and that is what makes it possible to enter the legislative arena with confidence and authority.

Staffing for Political Action

Although every member of the campus community is a potential source of political leadership, certain key personnel must understand and enjoy their special role in making the legislative program a success. The college relations director supervises much of the legislative program and must be a capable spokesman for the chief executive on all occasions, including meetings with the press or with legislators. No second-rate person can do this job, and the campus president must be adamant in finding a person with leadership qualities who has the respect of legislators.

Campus news writers and the news director are also obviously important as is a well-staffed office of alumni relations. What may not be as obvious is the need for a director of institutional research who understands the primacy of cost-benefit studies for program improvement, budget management, collective bargaining, and legislative information. Another key person in the legislative information program is the director of labor relations (personnel administrator). No unionized campus can afford to be without one regardless of whether the locus of formal negotiations is on campus or in a statewide office. Relationships between the campus executive and the union leadership may be the single most important avenue to legislative success. Administering the negotiated contract, settling grievances quickly and fairly, and communicating daily with union officials about political problems are basic to establishing and holding public confidence. After all, it was the inability of colleges to maintain internal unity during the sixties that literally destroyed centuries of public faith and myth built around scholarship, truth, and academic integrity. Shorn of this mythical power, campus executives of the seventies have no alternative but to build new legislative programs around current political realities.

Organizing Resources

Institutional Resources

The executive for some reason always starts by organizing those resources easiest to reach—his administrative colleagues. This is called "staffing" and has already been mentioned. Much more powerful for the purposes of political action, however, is to harness the political power of the several constituencies served by the institution. One of the institution's most important political constituencies is the campus governing board. Trustees will not organize themselves. They are politically appointed and enjoy "honorary" status in the academic community. That they are politically appointed gives them special significance, and the chief executive must see that they have a "political action" committee that works closely with the institution's community relations director who, in turn, must provide liaison with state functionaries and statewide organizations willing to support higher education. The trustees must be well informed about political realities influencing the quality and viability of the institution and must resolve to play an active and effective role in marshalling political support in behalf of the institution.

Where a campus has no board of trustees or where its membership is weak, the campus executive must become especially active in rectifying the situation. In the former case, the executive must appoint the most influential people who can be found to serve on campus advisory commissions, task forces, and special committees. In the latter case, the executive must build a network of support from local and regional people to influence the governor (or other appointing officials) to appoint highly respected and influential people as trustees. Failing this, the campus executive should have second thoughts about entering the legislative arena. An active, politically intelligent board is especially important to provide a sense of security for the president and his staff. Without the counsel and strong support of trustees, campus administrators are vulnerable to attack from every quarter. A weak board of trustees almost assures institutional political insignificance.

Neither will alumni organize themselves. Yet it is the county-by-county, region-by-region alumni organization that can not only raise funds but can effectively tackle every legislator of the state and can do so with impunity. Nothing is so impressive to a legislator as to see his constituents express organized concern for the welfare of their alma mater. ("College must have produced some benefits or these people wouldn't care!") Alumni, with more immunity than anyone else, can fight for such issues as low tuition and more tax support, if they really believe the issues are vital to the welfare of their college.

In contrast to alumni and trustees, students will organize themselves for effective political action, but only on momentary issues and for relatively short periods of time. The campus executive wishing to help students organize political clout for institutional support must provide ideas and inspiration without expecting too much in return. Students must be helped to collect student "activity fees" but given a free hand in their expenditure. To develop student understanding and "loyalty" to the academic enterprise, student leaders must be represented at all important meetings of advisory councils, long-range planning groups, budget planners, president's cabinet, trustees, faculty senate, and other similar groups. Especially useful for student understanding is to have student observers at union-employer meet-and-discuss (MAD) sessions. Student newspapers should be completely free from administrative-faculty influence for their "favorable" news stories to carry weight in the legislative halls. And students must be encouraged to join with students from other institutions in developing an independent, effective statewide and nationwide political lobby. No administrator should attempt to control student activity. Administratively controlled student groups are worthless as political instruments. At the same time, the administrator must expect to face some negative impact from student lobbies. But he must also be a statesman-like gambler believing that percentages will favor institutional purposes that cannot be successfully challenged by any one constituency. A campus president "presides" over all campus constituencies and must be equally interested in the welfare and rights of each.

Within the campus' civil community, no matter how small, resides a wealth of political support for the institution if properly marshalled. Most campus executives do a pretty good job of personally identifying with politically influential residents and of tapping their energies and support on special occasions. What they often do not do very well is keep the community well informed about detailed costs and benefits to the community and make them feel an integral part of the campus life. Unless local citizens have been psychologically prepared over a long period of time, their attempts to voice support for the local institution in a statewide political forum are likely to be feeble.

Although every president recognizes many sources of political potential, very few appear to recognize the new political realities of faculty and employee unions and especially their positive potential for joining in the support for broad institutional goals. This means that the campus president cannot be antiunion. Unions must be seen as potential political allies at the state and national levels. Experienced union leaders generally have more political clout with legislators than any group of college presidents. Relationships with local union leaders must be firm, fair, and open. Any other course leads to political disaster sooner or later. Faculty senates have no place in political activity, and every time they try to enter the political arena they are likely to create more harm and humor than institutional support. Faculty political activity should be left primarily to paid union leaders who are sophisticated in political maneuvering and relatively immune from political threats. After all, unions were born in the legislative womb.

Statewide Resources

Public college executives, partly from lack of experience and partly from fear of repercussions, usually encourage the state office of higher education to assume political leadership at the state level. This may also be true of private college presidents especially in northeastern states where a board of regents has traditionally protected the interests of private colleges (e.g., New York State). State officials also tend to see state politics as their special responsibility. By and large, however, state educational officers are ill-prepared for the realities of political life, have little experience in real politics, and usually mistake their person-to-person relationships with legislators and other state officials as politically effective. What they do not understand during their first year or so in office is that friendly relationships are no substitute for political clout. Political clout was simply lacking at the University of California when Governor Reagan decided to attack it during the late sixties. The University of Minnesota lacked political clout when the State Labor Board went against tradition in determining separate bargaining units for its several campuses. The State University of New York only once decided to go against the legislature's budget cuts (1965). In this one instance, trustees, faculty, alumni, and presidents from every corner of the state descended on legislators and the budget cut was restored. While I believe that state educational officers must strengthen their friendly relationships with the politicians, behind this friendship must be political clout organized at the grass-roots level. I also believe that state legislators want universities to be politically effective. Many legislators would put a higher priority on university needs if they thought it would aid rather than hurt their reelection to office.

The first statewide group to be organized by campus presidents should be a statewide organization of (1) public college executives, (2) private college administrators, and (3) a combination of these two. All exist now, but often in their weakest forms. One such organization, the American Association of University Administrators, exists at the national level, but it is a fledgling organization with no permanent full-time staff members. A national organization will always be weak until it has strong state-level units. Each state-level organization of administrators should have a full-time paid executive officer located at the capitol for purposes of direct liaison with legislators.

Campus presidents at public institutions must also insist that the chairman of the board of trustees, the president of the alumni association, and the president of the student association each set about helping to form an independent network of trustees, alumni, and students; that is, independent from the presidents, the chancellors, the central office, the politicians, and any other self-serving group. Each statewide group should have an independent lobby at the capitol. Unless presidents help initiate, lead, and sustain these independent forces, they cannot hope to preside when the organizations develop mutual assistance pacts.

Campus administrators through their statewide organization must meet with union leaders, suggest issues and parameters for cooperation, and invite cooperative efforts in securing legislative support for projects (e.g., budgets) that promote the objectives of both organizations simultaneously. Instant success is doubtful. What will happen immediately is more communication, and this eventually should lead to better campus relationships, fewer costly arbitrations, and eventually more political cooperation.

But campus administrators cannot stop there. They must work with ready-made organizations that have an indigenous interest in the vitality of higher education, such as the American Association of University Women, learned societies, women's groups, councils on the arts, and similar organizations at the state and national level. Many will claim immunity from political involvement, but it is amazing how they can stretch the definitions of "political" and "involvement" whenever the issue is sufficiently significant to their concerns.

In summary, much must be done before campus executives will feel their efforts have resulted in a more sensitive and receptive legislative attitude toward higher education. The first action must necessarily begin in the president's office with an awareness of the high priority to become involved in the political arena. The task will not be accomplished until administrators and constituencies both on and off the campus join ranks at all levels in a common desire to convince legislators and the general public of the paramount value of a strong and diversified higher educational system for all citizens.

References

1. *Special Report #17.* Staff Report of the Academic Collective Bargaining Information Service, 1818 R Street, N.W., Washington, D.C., May 1976.

2. Thomas R. Wolanin. "The National Higher Education Associations: Political Resources and Style." *Phi Delta Kappan*, October 1976, pp. 181-184.

3. James P. Begin. *Academics on Strike.* Rutgers University, New Jersey, 1975, pp. 110-121.

4. Louis U. Perelman. "On Limits to Growth, A Second Academic Revolution, and the President as Educational Leader." *The President as Educational Leader.* Washington, D.C.: Association of American Colleges, 1976, p. 41.

5. E.D. Duryea and Robert S. Fisk. "Collective Bargaining, The State University, and State Government in New York." *Faculty Bargaining, State Government and Campus Autonomy.* Denver, Colorado: A Joint Publication of the Pennsylvania State University and the Education Commission of the States, 1976, pp. 32-44.

Introduction to Chapter 8

Fritz H. Grupe and Alexander R. Cameron are both seasoned directors of institutional consortia in New York State. Increasingly the institutions composing their consortia are experiencing both the problems of financial exigency and pressures from the statewide Board of Regents and the state legislature for greater control over internal institutional decision making. Yet, neither Grupe nor Cameron find the potential of their regional organizations being fully realized. In fact, they suggest that some campuses seek to economize by terminating their membership!

Grupe and Cameron thus speak from experience and conviction when they state the case for voluntary regional cooperation. They describe the many ways consortia can help both public and private campuses economize, emphasizing that careful planning and commitment to cooperation are prerequisites. They discuss the barriers to cooperation with particular focus on the provincialism of campus leaders. And they discuss the potential for cooperation between regional consortia and statewide coordinating bodies. Like others in this volume, this chapter emphasizes the increasing need for campus-based leaders to look outward, as well as inward, in the battle for institutional survival.

8 Consortia and Financial Exigency: Promise or Premise?

Fritz H. Grupe and
Alexander R. Cameron

Several years ago the Newman Commission in its fresh and provocative review of the need for changes in postsecondary education commented, "Considering what needs to be done, we can afford the high cost of education, but not the low productivity."[1] During the same period, several Carnegie Commission reports suggested that a major goal for individual institutions should be the reduction of their anticipated projected expenditures by at least 20 percent.[2] Nothing in recent economic statistical projections for the general economy or for the financial state of postsecondary education provides evidence that institutions can relax in their search for more efficient operation.

The growth curve for consortia began its climb in the early 1960s, a time of expanding resources. Then, as now, there was insufficient recognition of the assertion that cooperation made economic sense. The implicit motivation for most cooperative ventures was to provide still another means for institutions to expand. Even today as retrenchment becomes a central fact of life, few college administrators are apparently giving any greater consideration to joint planning or programming as a primary or preferred alternative to insulated institutional decision making. There are, of course, periodic exceptions to this generalization, and there has been some general progress toward the awareness of common destinies; but the change has not generally been adequate to the demand. Awareness of the need for change is only the first step toward implementation. Institutions hope that they will be treated, for historic merit perhaps, more kindly than their neighbors. "Financial exigency may be happening now, but it can't possibly happen here," they seem to say.

Why aren't consortia becoming more active in the economizing of higher education? One supposes that institutions on the verge of demise would seek help from their peer institutions. They do not! One supposes that when colleges are forced to cut staff, they would determine first the extent to which various choices can be softened in their impact through intercollege exchanges of faculty and students. They do not! At a time when budgets are being trimmed, one would suppose that colleges might divide up "new growth" areas to encourage specialization and noncompetition in programs rather than participate in institutional imperialism. They do not! Indeed, observers are struck by the finding that consortia are as likely to be dropped as a part of institutional economies as they are to be used as a means of locating economies! The number of formal consortia, though still increasing annually, shows a high mortality rate, especially among newer cooperatives.

115

To be sure, all institutions are enmeshed in a web of cooperative relationships with other institutions. These relationships, numbering perhaps in the thousands across the country, range from day-long seminars involving only several faculty to the formally incorporated consortium, with a board of directors and a host of continuing programs.

Most of the arrangements, whether focusing on computers, faculty development, or student cross-registration, make economic as well as educational sense. An evaluation of the value of such ventures individually is easy and usually highly positive. Monies are saved, more effective programs are mounted, and a better educational process is fostered. In short, they have worked!

Why, then, is there an apparent contradiction between economy and cooperation? Consortia are successful; yet their achievements are short of the need for more substantive forms of cooperation on a scale commensurate with the financial pressures bearing down on all colleges. There are many reasons, some petty and some realistic. When crises requiring fast action occur, the cooperative process is slow and frustrating. Information needed is not always available. Each institution feels different pressures, sets different priorities, works from different philosophical bases, serves different masters, and reacts to different incentives. Most important, however, is that while institutions can easily find ways to do some programming together, they find it extremely difficult to plan strategically to work together. Even the word "cooperation" tends to favor the *easy-as-we-go* types of interaction that do not upset department chairmen, faculty senates, alumni associations, or anyone else with a divergent point of view.

Without a natural relationship to the planning process, interinstitutional cooperative programs can make only an accidental contribution. That is, when a consortial arrangement is merely superimposed on structures created by various members, isolated short- and long-range planning is bound to have minimal effect on a college's financial health. Although useful results may occur, reliance on happenstance is hardly a defensible way of managing institutions. The ability to choose between independent and consortial options requires that administrators secure an accurate perception of the cost objectives that can be met through intercollege collaboration, and that they set up in advance the preconditions that permit successful decisions to be made later on.

How Can Consortia Help?

The term "cooperation" is ambiguous and can include many different forms of actions taken to achieve many kinds of objectives.[3] Seldom will an institution admit that it is being uncooperative. Rather, it will assert that it seeks a different form of cooperation than its potential partners are seeking. Administrators must be expert in both the statement and the pursuit of cooperative objectives. In financial terms, the following suggests the objectives that can realistically be sought.

Cost Avoidance

The financial environment notwithstanding, there is no lack of interest in mounting new curricula, in obtaining more computer power, and in acquiring other special facilities. The pressure for growth has been overshadowed by financial concerns, but it has not abated. Indeed, academic expansion through diversification rather than retrenchment may be the only means of survival for some colleges. If an effective consortial relationship has been built, it should be possible to respond to many of these pressures is a fashion that is more creative than simply saying yes to high priorities and no to secondary items.

After all, most changes requested to represent legitimate and reasonable concerns. New programs of substance should not be approved or adopted without a review at least regionally, of the availability and accessibility of other comparable resources already present in nearby colleges. If a college can avoid investing in the creation of new faculty lines or can pilot test the depth of interest its faculty has for using computer terminals through the collaboration of a sister college, it will have realized a substantial gain. The West Central Wisconsin Consortium engages in just such an academic program review procedure, as does the Rochester Area Colleges in the Genesee Valley of upstate New York.

Cost Efficiency

Despite the most dynamic planning strategies, institutions must make long-range commitments to staff, facilities, and programs. Yet enrollments, student interests, national priorities, and faculty interests fluctuate. The institution is left with high- and low-enrollment classes, some under- and some overburdened faculty, and with both over- and underutilized instructional equipment. With appropriate agreements among campuses, it is possible to better balance combined demands with combined resources.

Cross-registration can move students out of high-demand courses into spaces available in lower demand courses. This process not only economizes the use of resources, but it also enhances greatly the choices open to the student. Faculty exchanges can also be used to match instructional talent with student interest. In a study of the financial effects of its cross-registration program, the Associated Colleges of the St. Lawrence Valley estimated that its member colleges had realized an enrichment of programs through cross-registration that approximated $750,000 in a single year. In the Rochester Area Colleges hundreds of students are receiving instruction at institutions other than their own in courses that would otherwise not be available to them. The process involves completion only of a simple one-page form, and there is no added expense to the student.

Cost Effectiveness

Some goals are simply beyond any likelihood of being implemented by an institution. A technological college cannot build a music department, and a community college generally cannot offer many specialized liberal arts courses. But there are students who may want these courses.

Again, through agreements like cross-registration and faculty exchanges, an accommodation of these limits can be made without requiring a single institution to bear all the attendant costs. This principle has long been demonstrated in the off-campus and study-abroad centers operated through the Associated Colleges of the Midwest and through a common registry of all part-time faculty in the Rochester area.

Avoidance of Destructive Competition

With the projected decline in the numbers of traditional age students and with a forecast of declining investment in higher education in many states, colleges cannot afford to engage in the unnecessary competition that was common in the past. Whether seeking entering freshmen from among graduating high school seniors, external funding from a region's possible donors, or "new clientele," colleges can adversely affect one another's investments and can injure their collective public image by unrestrained competition.

Without a satisfactory dialogue among them, institutions will find it difficult to attain or maintain a satisfactory control over these activities. A first step toward regional planning for continuing education was effectively implemented under funding through Title I of the Higher Education Act office of the New York State Education Department, as well as through the regional continuing education councils blanketing Virginia.

In the Genesee Valley of upstate New York, the Regents Regional Advisory Council in conjunction with the Rochester Area Colleges unanimously resolved that they would together review and react to the State Education Department on any program proposed by a member institution that requires master plan or charter amendment. The member institutions have also reaffirmed their intentions to advise each other of all program changes contemplated or under consideration at their respective schools.

Entry to Resource Centers

Consortia continue to be given priority in the awarding of many program operation grants. Realistically, funding agencies can see that it would be unwise to support the creation of overlapping community-based counseling services, duplicate comprehensive computer systems, or specialized curricula that serve identical audiences in a region. Funding agencies increasingly look for projects that involve the participation of all a region's colleges that have legitimate interest in the new activity. On the agency's part, this priority makes sense because it limits the likelihood of destructive competition and it recognizes that few individual institutions may have the commitment or the resources for large-scale projects. For this reason federal and philanthropic organizations have supported a student volunteer program in the Associated Colleges of the St. Lawrence Valley. The project coordinator brings volunteers from the four campuses to some thirty-five social agencies. By consolidating their efforts, the project supports professional staff assistance for recruitment, orientation, training, and supervision. For institutions, consortial grants mean that they have no choice but to cooperate if they wish to participate. Single institutions cannot meet the minimal criteria to gain entry into the support base.

The Fund for the Improvement of Postsecondary Education, Title I of the Higher Education Act, and the Developing Institutions Program of the U.S. Office of Education are three programs that have a distinct inclination toward the support of consortial arrangements.

Resource Amplification

By making its operations more efficient, an institution can use some of its resources in a different fashion. In the use of these funds and in its other investments, the college undertakes to provide services that go further than they might have. For instance, if two colleges coordinate their library and audio-visual acquisition, not only do they encourage fuller utilization of their holdings, but they are able to obtain additional nonduplicative holdings that they could not have secured otherwise.

A recent pilot study by the staff of Rochester Area Colleges discovered duplication in orders of high-cost, highly specialized, and limited-use serials by member institutions and in turn recommended coordination of purchases to expand acquisitions. Additionally, through joint film purchases, RAC institutions enjoy the use of expensive series like the *Ascent of Man* at a cost to each individual college of only several hundred dollars.

The same principle holds true of many staff appointments. Five Colleges,

Inc., in Massachusetts, has been able to develop five faculty joint appointments that annually permit the institutions to bring in specialized talents that otherwise would not have been possible to offer. The Worcester Consortium for Higher Education assembled a new health administration option by drawing on existing course offerings and by adding several new counseling and internship experiences.

Examples of joint ventures that demonstrate unmistakable efficiencies could be cited at length. The utility of establishing a new organizational structure need not mean that automatic savings will result, though the probabilities of doing so are increased. In fact, it is predictable that without thoughtful planning and without a sincere effort to engage in intercampus negotiations, a new consortium could result in increased expenditures for the member institutions.

There are now well over 100 formally incorporated, multipurpose consortia. Although they vary considerably in their characteristics, many of their programs are transferable in concept. Assistance can be obtained through the newly created Council for Interinstitutional Leadership in locating those programs in which real financial and educational benefits can be effected. Consortia do function well when institutions approach their problems in a sophisticated and knowledgeable manner.

Making Cooperation Work: The Critical Role of Campus Leaders

Interinstitutional cooperation is a concept that has a definite role in a period of financial exigency. There is no doubt that the consortial relationship can be made more innovative, more productive, more adequate to the constraints of financial exigency. The key to making the consortium more effective remains, however, a responsibility of institutional administrators and faculty. Outside agencies can and will respond to demonstrably more effective campus initiatives with encouragement and financial support. How can institutional administrators who agree that more must be done facilitate the emergence of cross-campus programs and activities? The following concepts are basic to interinstitutional cooperation.

Campus Presidents as Initiators of Consortial Arrangements

Institutions of higher education are collegial at least in one sense. Top-echelon administrators help in showing the way toward cooperation by staying visible as initiators, not just as "watchers," of the consortial movement. Top administrators must personally participate in establishing a new consortium and must continually nurture and support its development. If a relationship already exists, the same individuals should be the primary originators of new ideas and the primary evaluators of joint ventures to assure that inter- and intra*institutional* priorities are being addressed.

Dr. Paul Miller, President of the Rochester Institute of Technology, has stated:

The consortium is an important entity in our midst, it is making reasonable progress, but we can do better. I say "we" for I feel that whatever happens to it is a question of what *the presidents* desire to achieve in order to help them make good on their own institutional goals. In short, our problem, if we have one, is not the absence of possibilities, but rather how we mount sufficient will to make [the consortium] a servant of our individual and collective needs.[4]

Top administrators should also expect, recognize, and reward staff for initiating cooperative ventures. Faculty cannot be expected to take on the inconvenience of voluntarily traveling to another campus and academic departments cannot be expected to coordinate their course sequences (even if major institutional gains are realized) if no incentive is given to them.

A call for incentives need not mean increased salaries. But contributions that aid the institution should be supported in some way.

1. Are departments asked to report on their cooperative efforts?
2. Will they be given reasons for accommodating the interests of students from other campuses?
3. Are administrative obstacles to academic cooperation sought and eliminated as evidence of institutional commitment?
4. Are departments queried on the extent to which they studied cooperative ventures before proposing new appointments or curricula?

If questions like these cannot be answered affirmatively, significant levels of cooperation are unlikely.

Campus Presidents as Facilitators of Communication

Stereotypes never improve communications. Simplistic assessments of what another institution is or is not, can or cannot do, may reduce the need for choices that involve other institutions. But oversimplifications of this kind will not help the decision maker to find economies through cooperation. It is essential, therefore, that campus chief executives articulate to other colleges their future institutional goals and the means for their achievement. Once institutional commitments have been made to computer hardware, new staff, or new curricula, cooperation is forced to a predictably low level. The insurmountable problems of trying to match incompatible television units or of attempting to elicit interest in multicampus teaching assignments when a new instructor has already been "captured" by a department are indicative of the difficulties inherent in an absence of preliminary institutional agreements.

Each institution in a consortium must not only define its own objectives but must also assist actively in deciding what programs and objectives the consortium must pursue. The members must clarify the areas in which they can collectively focus sufficient attention and allocate needed resources to bring about a change. In the Rochester Area Colleges, college presidents meet annually for a day-long working session to set goals and discuss consortium programs. (This meeting is in addition to the presidents' attendance at quarterly board meetings and at various consortium committee sessions.) A member of the Board of Directors, usually the president or a trustee of one of the colleges, exercises oversight responsibility for every major project or program that Rochester Area Colleges undertakes. It is not coincidental that enthusiasm for the consortium runs high on those campuses whose presidents actively participate.

Voluntary Cooperation and Statutory Coordination

A number of observers have commented on the simultaneous growth of academic consortia and statewide coordinating boards. Consortia created voluntarily by colleges and universities and state coordinating boards created by statute via legislation both seek to make the utilization of limited resources committed to education more effective and efficient. They both seek to make the system of higher education more responsive to less parochial needs and objectives.

There are, however, important distinctions between the two organizations. On the one hand, cooperation relies on the voluntary participation of institutions and not upon control of funding, coercion, or external statutory control. Institutions retain the essential power and autonomy to decide for themselves which activities are consistent with their goals.

Coordination, by contrast, involves a third party that has the ultimate responsibility to foster the changes its political constituencies seek. Although campus support for these changes may be present, campus agreement is not totally required. Initiatives can come from outside sources. Nor are these initiatives necessarily congruent with the perceived goals off the campuses. Ostensibly, the coordinating body offers an avenue for bringing the public interest to bear on the growth and development of the higher education system through statutory and fiscal control. Coordination assumes that a statutory power exists to enforce the processes of planning, review, and budgeting.

Critics of consortia have pointed to the shortcomings of the voluntary cooperation movement. They cite the replacement of voluntary statewide coordinating mechanisms by statutory boards during the 1960s as further evidence of the limitations of cooperation. But the parallel is not exact, and to evaluate one organization by the other is to miss their distinctive purposes. By and large, consortia have been created by their members to fulfill a role that is unabashedly partial to its members. This role may overlap the concerns of coordinating bodies, but not entirely.

There is no reason for conflict between the voluntary and statutory bodies. In some states, most notably Illinois, Virginia, New York, Pennsylvania, and California, the state coordinating units have begun to blend the two bases for decision making through the formation of regional planning councils. To some extent several of these statewide efforts were begun by the coordinating boards as a reflection of their belief (partially warranted) that purely voluntary consortia are not able to operate with the speed and the decisiveness that the times seem to require. How successfully the methods previously applied only to public institutions can be applied to combinations of public and private institutions remains to be determined.

There is little doubt, however, that destinies of individual institutions will come increasingly to reflect shared problems. Consortia are the first-line opportunity open to these institutions, public and private alike, to demonstrate their good faith and ability to engage voluntarily in joint planning and meaningful decision making. There are those who are quite vocal in asserting that since the past history of voluntary cooperatives has failed to eliminate needless duplication and competition that are often blatantly obvious to even the general public, a more authoritative approach is in order.

Advocates of voluntary cooperation must admit that, though the consortium movement has continued to progress, questions can be raised about its speed and direction. The potential role of consortia is, as it has been since the 1960s, of considerable potential value. Colleges must decide, and they must decide soon, whether the necessity for cooperation will be taken as a promise that remains ever unfulfilled or as a premise that serves as an effective guide to future actions.

If the historical progress of consortia has not convinced institutions that cooperation is inevitable, a quick analysis of the future environment for higher education should. Far more can be accomplished. Far more will be expected. The building of a successful consortium or the development of a complementary network of relationships in a variety of contexts for a single institution is not a once-and-for-all matter. A good deal of thought, effort, and interaction are needed to sustain a healthy network of institutions. "Matrix management" is a talent administrators will have to advance substantially in the near future.

References

1. Task Force (Frank Newman, Chairman). *Report on Higher Education.* U.S. Department of Health, Education, and Welfare: Office of Education. Washington, D.C.: U.S. Government Printing Office, 1971, p. 28.

2. Carnegie Commission on Higher Education. *Priorities for Action: Final Report.* New York: McGraw-Hill, 1973, p. 64.

3. Paper presented to presidents of the Rochester Area Colleges in January 1976.

4. Fritz H. Grupe. *Managing Interinstitutional Change.* Potsdam, N.Y.: Associated Colleges of the St. Lawrence Valley, 1975, pp. 70-76.

Introduction to Chapter 9

Centralization is occurring at a progressively greater rate in postsecondary education. Public multicampus systems, unionization, regional consortia, state and federal aid programs, to name a few, thrust power off individual campuses and upward. Financial exigency is destined to become another force calling for a more centralized approach to resource allocation and utilization.

Patrick M. Callan and Richard W. Jonsen combine their backgrounds in public and private education, respectively, to examine the role statewide planning should play in helping institutions adjust to new conditions. While they opt for independent coordinating agencies that leave substantial autonomy to individual campuses and regional consortia, they readily admit that the tensions surrounding decisions of these agencies generate tremendous political forces capable of threatening delicate neutrality. Once a coordinating agency becomes known as the handmaiden of a particular sector of postsecondary education, its effectiveness is ended. Callan and Jonsen examine the functions statewide planning agencies will be asked to perform in the days ahead, note the precarious political environment in which they are to function, and then discuss a number of issues and problems that must be addressed if coordination is to be a feasible alternative to state control. Of particular interest to both public and private administrators will be their examination of the role of statewide coordinating agencies vis-à-vis private and proprietary institutions.

Planning Retrenchment: The State Role

Patrick M. Callan and
Richard Jonsen

Postsecondary education administrators seeking to interrelate more effectively with their environments must understand the functions and the structure of state planning and coordinating agencies. Because these agencies are likely to acquire increasing significance in the affairs of all institutions of higher education, this chapter is designed to acquaint administrators with the major elements of agency functions, their political dynamics, and the issues of greatest current significance to them.

The emergence of state coordinating agencies as important forces in postsecondary education in the United States coincides with the period of the most rapid expansion in the history of American higher education. There were two coordinating boards in the United States in 1940; there were three in 1950, eleven in 1960, and twenty-eight by 1974.[1] The rise of coordination accompanied trends toward universal postsecondary opportunities and the dominance of public postsecondary institutions.

The creation of these agencies was a recognition of the increased interdependence of institutions, the rapidly growing magnitude of state resources required by higher education, the necessity for more rational allocation of functions and resources among institutions, and the inability of the voluntary interinstitutional bodies which had existed in many of these states to make effective and timely decisions regarding allocations of functions and resources.

The functions of coordinating boards also reflected their establishment during an era of dramatic growth. As a rule, coordinating boards were charged either explicitly or implicitly with assisting state governments in assimilating this growth in an orderly and efficient manner, developing rational policies for accommodating an ever-expanding pool of students and resources. Accordingly, the state master plans produced by these agencies tended to be blueprints for expansion. Viewed from this perspective, coordination was essentially a state response to a particular set of problems and issues in a particular era, orchestrating expansion during a period of unprecedented growth.

The opposite kind of problem now confronts statewide agencies: how to adjust to diminishing resources. In this chapter we explore the role of coordinating boards in facilitating this adjustment. We begin by reviewing different patterns of coordination.

A Variety of Patterns

There is no standard form of statewide coordination of postsecondary education. On the contrary, there is a bewildering variety of legal authorities, structures, scope and functions. Millard[2] divides state postsecondary agencies into three broad types: governing boards with responsibility for all public institutions (11) or all senior public institutions (7); coordinating boards created by constitutions or statutes (30); boards created by governors' executive orders (11). The overlap is primarily in the last category; some agencies created by executive order (in response to the Education Amendments of 1972 and their section "1202" mandating statewide planning) have planning responsibilities and parallel existing government agencies of one of the other types. The agencies were established under boards to assure their independence of partisan politics and of the institutions they were to coordinate. The legislation creating the agencies and boards limited the authority of the coordinating structures, attempting to strike a balance between centralized planning, which has always been somewhat suspect in the United States, and the absolute autonomy of the institution which often leads to chaotic and wasteful duplication and competition in periods of financial stringency.

Adding somewhat to the confusion created by the varieties of structures, authorizations, scope and functions, are the differences among these agencies in the actual power they possess with respect to postsecondary education. Some agencies have acquired a good deal of actual power despite their supposedly advisory role. Others, even though accorded constitutional or statutory authority, have been less influential. The key ingredients are the political dynamics of the states, the leadership of the agency heads, and the relative power of the institutions themselves.

Retrenchment and Coordinating Board Functions

The most important functions that state postsecondary agencies perform are planning, program approval and review, and budget review. In the performance of these functions and in the relative responsibility held by the agency (as between, say, approval and advice), the agencies also vary widely.

Planning and Retrenchment

The planning function, even though the least specific, is pivotal, especially with regard to retrenchment. In its broadest sense, planning may include the establishment and differentiation of institutional mission and scope, the identification of new institutional sites, the distribution of resources and personnel among institutions and systems, the identification of emerging needs, and similar tasks. It also includes the most general and critical of planning functions—setting system-level or statewide goals, priorities, and criteria for evaluation. These planning functions bear significantly on the other coordination functions of budget and program review.

Under conditions of growth, statewide planning involved determinating system size, identifying new resources to accomodate that size, and allocating resources among systems and institutions.

Under conditions of decline, statewide planning plays an opposite but perhaps more critical role. Instead of allocating increasing resources among competing claims, steady or even declining resources must be allocated among claimants in some order of priority. New programs may have to be undertaken at the expense of existing ones. At the extreme, institutions may have to be closed. These enormously unpopular aspects of planning are precisely those that will establish the leadership role of statewide agencies but, at the same time, may exacerbate the tension between them and their constituent institutions. The resolution of this tension is a critical determinant of the future course of the statewide agency.

Within the statewide planning function, the scope of postsecondary education will be identified. Thus, the range of clients and the range of institutions to serve them will be narrow or broad as a result of the basic attitudes and decisions planners take.

Within the statewide planning function, the priorities given to competing goals of postsecondary education will be fixed; the criteria that public policy makers can use to evaluate achievement of those goals and to review competing applications for resources can be established; and the shape and significance of emerging needs will be determined.

Program Review

A second function of state postsecondary agencies, one which has been getting increased attention, is program review and approval. Under system expansion, program review and even program approval seem to be perfunctory. Under retrenchment they are not, because they bring the process of coordination down to the level where it appears to conflict directly with institutional authority. Thus, in New York, the State University of New York (SUNY) has challenged the authority of the Regents to review doctorgal programs and require their elimination. Barak and Berdahl[3] observe that whereas nineteen coordinating and governing agencies (out of twenty-four) had program approval authority in 1960, thirty-eight (out of forty-seven) appeared to have such authority in 1975. The increased exercise of this authority involves not only political issues such as the encroachment (from the standpoint of the institution) of the state agency upon institutional "autonomy," but also some difficult technical questions related to evaluation itself: criteria, their validation, sufficient evidence, accurate data—issues that always surround educational evaluation.

In one sense, what these political and technical problems illustrate is the difficulty of shifting from a traditional and relatively "free market," in which institutions are allowed to compete with few constraints for clients and resources, to a "system" in which there is some centralized coordination of allocation decisions involving both clientele and resources. Allocation of programs is central to this shift, because it implies that not every institution may undertake every function. Some allocation decisions will be made not at the level of the institution, but at the level of the state coordinating agency which will mediate between conflicting claims for programs, clients, and resources. Although the private sector involvement in formal program review currently is slight, it is likely to become more common as the development and expansion of programs becomes increasingly perceived in a competitive market.

Budget Review

In budgeting, just as in program review, the authority and scope of coordinating agency functions vary among the states. The responsibilities range from developing a consolidated budget request for all public institutions in the state (nineteen states), to conducting reviews and making recommendations on each institutional budget request (five states), to recommending formulas (one state), to no role at all in the budget process (three states).[4] For agencies that have budget functions, a primary consideration is to assure that the statewide plans, policies, and priorities are reflected in the budgetary process. Unless budgeting and planning are linked, even the best state plans are doomed to futility.

It seems clear that budgetary review is likely to become a more significant function of postsecondary agencies. The alternative of more decentralized control, at the institutional or system level, seems extraordinarily unlikely in the face of fiscal constraints. As funds tighten, resources must be reviewed more rather than less as competition for them increases. A third alternative is centralization of the budget function to other offices—executive budget offices or legislative committees. This course would seem less palatable and, indeed, less desirable educationally since less sensitivity to the educational issues is likely to be evident at these levels. At the same time, the influence of political partisanship is likely to grow under such conditions.

The Political Position of the Coordinating Agency

From a political standpoint, the position of the coordinating board may be the most delicate of any of the participants in the process. The very attribute that gives the coordinating agency its cause for existence and its credibility—independence from the political arms of the state government and from the educational institutions—makes its position difficult. In the environment in which the agency operates, all the major participants can call upon political constituencies. It plays a middle role that requires sensitivity to the concerns of both government and the higher education community. Yet it must maintain its independence; it cannot, either in fact or in perception, be the uncritical advocate of a single set of interests. Similarly, although the agency is in the middle, it cannot be either a simple information exchange or mediator. Although a passive approach may provide some short-run insulation from attacks and controversy, the long-range effect would be to undermine the agency's purposes. In short, the agency must determine and enunciate a definable posture.

The contributions that coordinating agencies can make to the public policy process stem from their ability to bring to bear a long-range, holistic, and comprehensive assessment of needs and resources based on accurate data and careful analysis. It is the quality of the advice, recommendations, and decisions that the agency renders rather than the degree of consensus it develops that, in the last analysis, determines its contribution.

Perhaps regrettably, but certainly understandably, the tendency of many institutional and political participants in the public policy arena is to support the need for interdependence in the abstract, but in the specific case to attack positions that conflict with their perceived interests. The inevitable presence of significant interests in controversial issues (definitionally) places coordinating boards in the crucible when announcing their recommendations. Crucibles tend to represent the type of world that coordinating agencies and boards were created to live in. Coordinating agencies must sometimes introduce into the public dialogue ideas that may not win immediate acceptance and in so doing become lightning rods, drawing energies to the decision-making process.

It is apparent from the foregoing that the leadership role of the coordinating agency is one that when exercised may well lead to tensions and conflict. This is especially true in an environment of stability or retrenchment. It is difficult for an institution to accommodate to the realities of stability or decline. Americans have been socialized to expect regular increases in resources, and college and university presidents are no exceptions. Their expectations may have been shaped by environments in which denial was relative. Under such conditions, unhappiness was also relative, usually caused by budget increases smaller for some than for others. Perhaps of more importance, their legitimacy as institutional leaders is related in some measure to their ability to provide increases at budget time, something less likely in the present environment. From the perspective of the general public, and for better or worse, the coordinating agency may not be subject to such internal pressures and can recommend allocations and reallocations of resources to institutions and programs according to its perception of statewide priorities.

If financial exigency and the resulting public policy decisions constitute one dimension of the political environment of state coordination, the growing complexity of the political governmental process itself is another. Governors and state budget offices have expanded their staffs and their analytical capability in higher education, bringing about parallel increases in legislative staff capabilities. State government is now equipped to analyze, scrutinize, and evaluate higher education, much to the consternation of institutions which find themselves frequently deluged with requests from multiple sources.

For the coordinating agency, the increased complexity and sophistication of the state government environment has at least two significant consequences. First, it must expect that its work will be subjected to more critical analysis than would have occurred in the past. Second, it must have its role distinguished from other agencies and staffs involved in studying and making recommendations in the area of higher education. The specific elements of that role definition will be worked out in each state based upon legal and historical considerations. However, it is essential that every state coordinating agency have the capacity for independent policy analysis. The statewide planning function is central, and it is a function that neither the political nor institutional leaders have the resources or the insulation from constituent pressure to accomplish. By virtue of its position in the midst of conflicting forces, the agency is able to wield influence, through planning and analysis, on both the more general political interests and upon higher education. The success of the agency in this sensitive role is dependent upon its capability for leadership—largely a political task—as well as upon technical competence and vision in attacking problems and issues.

Issues and Problems

Improvement of Statewide Planning

In most states the effectiveness of state planning could be improved in regard to processes, outcomes, and implementation.

The planning process has developed two important attributes critical to its success in the ensuing environment of resource scarcity. First, the process must be continuous and participatory. With respect to the first of these, both the technical and political dimensions of planning should be fully recognized. The imperfections of planning technology and the uncertainties of societal and educational futures create a necessity for continuous planning. This means focusing on a few carefully chosen and well-defined issues at a time, within the context of a long-range or strategic framework. Strategic planning should occur at longer intervals and should involve establishing goals, charting long-range directions, and identifying the most important public policy issues on the horizon. The day of the master plan that attempted to combine all the planning to be done in a state—short-range and strategic—in one massive effort at specified intervals is undoubtedly over. Most coordinating agencies lack the resources for this kind of effort. And the sensitivity of the issues in a time of severe resource constraint makes it difficult to deal with them all at one time without overloading the plan politically and creating insurmountable opposition to the entire planning effort.

Secondly, it cannot be overemphasized that effective planning is a *consultative process* that draws much of its legitimacy and vitality from the participation of the external and internal constituencies of postsecondary education. The mechanisms for participation may include formal consultation, public hearings, advisory committees, questionnaires, and other devices. Constituent groups will include institutional administrators, faculty, students, and governing boards, as well as statewide interest groups such as unions, student lobbies, other planning agencies, and the public, in addition to the political leadership the state agency formally relates to: governors' offices, legislative committees, etc. Individual and institutional opinions should be solicited on issues to be taken up in the planning process; opportunities for reactions to preliminary findings and recommendations should also be provided. Without this kind of (over)due process, the credibility of planning efforts will be suspect—and it should be suspect—regardless of the technical quality of the plan.

The outcomes of this fluid process must be specified in concrete terms. The palpable outcome is the plan itself—whether strategic or tactical. In evaluating the outcome, the first question that should be raised is whether the plan identifies the major policy issues facing the state. The greatest danger in planning is perhaps not error (which can be corrected at a later time in a continuous process), but irrelevance. Planners must guard against the tendency to write a plan for the *last* ten years, to prevent a recurrence of past errors. But if plans look only backward and not forward, the issues addressed may be the reverse of those most relevant to the present and the future. For example, instead of trying to determine the maximum practical sizes of campuses and programs (an important issue in the 1960s), it may now be necessary to determine the minimum critical sizes. By the same token, because an era of difficult priority-setting is upon us, plans should specify the criteria for state support of institutions and programs, thereby creating a conceptual framework and an informational base for future program and budget reviews.

Plans should identify the agency responsible for implementing each recommendation and the information that will be collected to monitor and evaluate implementation. They should also include provisions for amendment and systematic review, specification of the relationship of the state plan to institutional planning efforts, explicit statements of the underlying assumptions and principles not dealt with. There should also be a review of state funding—present and future—and administrative policies to assure that at least they do not constitute disincentives to implementation of the recommendations. Whenever possible, incentives should be defined and provided.

A good deal of plan implementation will occur in the reviews of proposed and existing programs and through budget analysis. This is why it is so important that the plan specify the criteria and information to be used, particularly in the evaluation of programs. Otherwise, evaluations will take place on an ad hoc basis with the ground rules poorly understood by participants and with decisions made on primarily ad hoc and political bases. For program and budget review, it will be disastrous to attempt to create the criteria and procedures and to make difficult decisions at the same time: the plan must put the mechanisms in place prior to any type of review process.

Centralization versus Decentralization

Obviously, one of the recurring issues in higher education, and especially in the context of statewide planning, is that of centralization. The notion of institutional autonomy is a cherished myth in American higher education. It tends to be supported by the reality of a relatively free market in higher education, which is unique to the United States. The preservation of institutional independence, as statewide planning and coordination become more powerful and extensive, is both a political and an educational issue. It is a political issue for the obvious reason that power and resources are at stake. It is an educational issue because the extent to which vitality and innovation depend upon a degree of autonomy is a real, if somewhat indeterminate, factor in higher education. Institutions need to have a good deal of autonomy in curricular matters—student and faculty selection and program organization and reorganization. Where that autonomy becomes seriously circumscribed is at the level of development of new programs, determination of productivity levels (as these are the result of budgeting formulas), and overall determination of mission, and levels of financial support.

The tensions are bound to increase as coordinating boards exercise their authority for programs and budgets. As this happens, it will be important to prevent the self-generating bureaucratic processes from inevitable tendencies toward overcentralization. This will involve (1) maintenance and definition of proper academic decisions, on curriculum and personnel, at the institutional level, (2) preservation of maximum budget flexibility, even flexibility to make judgments about the proper place for cuts, and the need for internal reallocation of resources, at the institutional level, and (3) the encouragement, even under fiscal exigency, of innovative proposals, at the institutional level, so that grass-roots vitality and imagination can be sustained and nourished.

Private and Proprietary Institutions

The Education Amendments of 1972 and the provision they contained for statewide planning (section 1212)[5] have changed the nature of coordination in at least two important ways. First, planning itself, as seen in the light of federal policy at least, has come to encompass a more comprehensive set of postsecondary institutions than it did previously. Under the provisions of section 1202 of the Education Amendments of 1972, planning agencies must be broadly and equitably representative of postsecondary education. The private sector has been included in a more specific way in the setting of postsecondary educational policy, in theory, if not always in fact. Second, the extension of federal student aid programs to students enrolled in proprietary institutions has, with the broadening of the planning scope, included such institutions for the first time in the definition of postsecondary education. Private sector needs and problems were recognized by some state policies and programs prior to 1972. A number of state agencies had paid some attention to the private sector in their comprehensive plans, some had initiated separate studies of the status and needs of the private sector, and, more concretely, a number of states (such as New York, Pennsylvania, Illinois, and New Jersey) had developed programs in direct or indirect financial support of the private sector. These included programs of state student-aid grants, which, in many cases flow largely to students in independent colleges and universities, and in seven states programs of direct financial support to private institutions.

The problems in the private sector had become accentuated as states developed more or less comprehensive systems of public higher education which, at relatively low tuition prices, made recruitment of students more and more difficult for private colleges and universities. Because private colleges depend largely upon tuition income, recruitment problems are increasingly critical. Scholarship programs provide some relief. Institutional aid programs recognize that problems persist even if enrollments hold up.

One effect of these programs of support, however, has been to draw the private sector more closely into statewide planning, an effect not welcomed by all private institutions. This phenomenon also raises important policy issues about the basis for such support. What is the public function performed by the private colleges, and is their operation totally in the public interest? What are the specific governmental purposes served by support to private institutions? Where such support is given, what are the reciprocal responsibilities of private institutions? These questions may not be solved on the theoretical level, but they are certain to be resolved operationally by legislation, state administrative decisions, and the courts. It seems quite likely that if state support increases, private colleges and universities will be seen as part of the public system of postsecondary education by state planners and will become increasingly subject to state requirements, for example, in the submission of data. On a more controversial level, if state support takes the form of institutional subsidies, independent institutions of postsecondary education are likely to be brought under the authority of state agencies concerning activities traditionally under their autonomous control, such as the initiation of new programs. Private college administrators need to be aware of these trends and should be in close contact with those state officials who have a voice in the shaping of policies that will increasingly affect the private sector.

Incorporation of the proprietary sector into state planning and coordination may pose even greater problems. Though student-aid programs at the federal level are open to students attending proprietary institutions, such is not the case in most states. This is likely to become a significant issue. The proprietary sector is much less organized at the state level, however, so that its voice is likely to be less clear than that of the independent sector (though perhaps more unified). It is also less well known in the total scope of its operation, in its effects, and in the degree to which it competes with vocational-technical education operated by the public sector (principally community colleges and vocational-technical institutions). Much more needs to be known about these institutions individually and in the aggregate before satisfactory inclusion in planning can take place.

At the very least, states and state higher education agencies must encourage genuine involvement of the private and proprietary sectors in planning and policy deliberations, build clear and cogent bases for policies and programs involving the private sector, and maintain rational and well-supported policies that specify the mechanisms of accountability involving private institutions.

The Future of Statewide Coordination

The major issue regarding the future of coordination is whether an essentially decentralized approach which attempts to achieve cohesiveness and accountability through planning and policy analysis can meet the needs of the states under conditions of financial exigency. The basic difference between coordinating boards and consolidated governing boards is that the former leave the responsibility for management and operation of multicampus systems and individual institutions to boards of trustees and presidents. Whether this delicate and somewhat fragile approach can be maintained at a time when scarcity of resources increases the interdependence of policy decisions and intensifies the pressures for accountability depends upon the sensitivity and astuteness of the coordinating boards and their staffs, the commitment of the institutions of higher education to maintaining the mechanism despite short-run disagreements, and the political environment in each state. The pattern in recent years is that when coordination is perceived as ineffective, the tendency of governors and legislators has been to move to more rather than less centralization, often away from coordinating boards to consolidated governing boards. It is likely that the private sector would fare less well under consolidated governing boards, which tend, understandably, to emphasize their authority and responsibilities to public institutions.

Coordinating agencies, like the institutions of higher education, will be severely tested in the late 1970s and 1980s. The essence of the test is not whether they can survive but whether they can effectively serve the important public purposes for which they were established. In the final analysis, statewide coordination should be judged by its ability to bring about improvements in the rational ordering of higher education programs to operate more efficiently and to better serve its clients.

References

1. Robert O. Berdahl. "Problems in Evaluating Statewide Boards." In *Evaluating Statewide Boards: New Directions for Institutional Research*, Robert O. Berdahl (ed.). San Francisco: Jossey-Bass, 1975.

2. Richard M. Millard. *State Boards of Higher Education.* ERIC/Higher Education Report #4. Washington, D.C., 1976.

3. Robert J. Barak and Robert O. Berdahl. "Final Report SHEEO/ECS-IEP Program Review Project." Denver, Colorado, August 1976.

4. Millard, *State Boards of Higher Education.*

5. Education Amendments of 1972.

About the Contributors

George W. Angell is Director of the Academic Collective Bargaining Information Service in Washington, D.C. He has 20 years of experience as a college president. As an author, consultant and speaker, he has added considerably to the available research and knowledge on collective bargaining in higher education. He has also acted as consultant to legislative committees responsible for educational legislation.

J. Victor Baldridge is on the staff of the Higher Education Research Institute in Los Angeles and is a member of the UCLA Graduate School of Education. As a former administrator at California State University, Fresno, he has had practical experience in dealing with academic innovation and evaluation of new programs. And while a faculty member at Stanford University, he directed the Stanford Project on Academic Governance, a national study of college decision making and innovation. He has published a number of books on academic governance.

Patrick M. Callan is executive coordinator of the Washington State Commission on Higher Education. He has directed master plan studies for California and Montana, which resulted in the *Report of the Joint Committee on the Master Plan for Higher Education* (1973) in California and *Final Report: Montana Commission on Postsecondary Education* (1974).

William J. Collard is Staff Associate with the National Center for Higher Education Management Systems. He has extensive experience as a systems analyst, instructor and consultant.

James Farmer currently designs management information systems for higher education through Systems Research, Inc. In addition, he has extensive service experience at the State and national level.

Stephen Finn is assistant to the Provost at The Ohio State University. He received the MBA degree from the School of Business Administration at Fordham University, where he concentrated on managerial structure and activity in the public sector. He has done extensive work on the development and implementation of managerial support systems for responding effectively to academic collective bargaining.

William Proctor, President of Flagler College in St. Augustine, Florida, received the Ph.D. from Florida State University where he held a variety of administrative positions. He is Vice Chairman of the Independent College and University Association of Florida.

Fritz H. Grupe is the Executive Director of the Associated Colleges of the St. Lawrence Valley. He has written a number of articles on interinstitutional cooperation as well as a book on consortium administration. He serves as a member of the Board of Directors for the Council for Interinstitutional Leadership.

Alexander R. Cameron has been Executive Director of the Rochester Area Colleges since 1972. This consortium is unique because its membership includes nine private institutions, three units of the public State University of New York (SUNY), and three public community colleges—all located in the eight-county region of the Genesee Valley of Western New York. Dr. Cameron has served in several administrative positions prior to joining the Rochester Area Colleges, including Assistant to former SUNY Chancellor Samuel Gould and Vice President for Administration at SUNY-Brockport.

Richard M. Jonsen is director of the Project on State Policy and Independent Higher Education at Education Commission of the States. He is on leave from Syracuse University where he is assistant dean of the School of Education and assistant professor of higher education.

John G. Harrison has served as Director of Information Systems for the California State University and College system and is Chief of Information Systems for the State of California.

David Leslie earned the Ph.D. from the Pennsylvania State University and is Associate Professor of Education in the Center for the Study of Higher Education at the University of Virginia. He has conducted funded research in collective bargaining, law and education, and conflict management. His more than thirty articles and professional papers have dealt with such diverse topics as due process for students and faculty members, principles of grievance systems, collective bargaining, and academic governance. He is active in campus governance at the University of Virginia and in a number of national professional organizations.

About the Editors

Frank R. Kemerer is a graduate of Stanford University, with a Ph.D. in educational administration and a law minor through the Stanford Law School. His specialities include educational administration, educational law, and organizational theory. Dr. Kemerer is the Assistant to the President of the State University of New York College of Arts and Science at Geneseo and also teaches courses in Constitutional law and student civil liberties. He is the senior author of *Unions on Campus: A National Study of the Consequences of Faculty Bargaining* (San Francisco: Jossey-Bass, 1975), a monograph on the same subject for the National Association of Independent Schools, and numerous articles and essays related to both higher and secondary education.

Ronald P. Satryb is Assistant to the President for Employee Relations and Assistant Vice President for Business Affairs at the State University of New York College of Arts and Science at Geneseo, New York. He earned the Ed.D. in higher educational administration from the University of Virginia. His experience in college administration over the past decade includes student affairs, business affairs, and employee relations. His numerous articles and speeches include grievance processing, discipline, personnel procedures, budgeting and due process. He has, by virtue of his position at SUNY-Geneseo, directly experienced the challenge of developing effective retrenchment procedures.